AUSTEN

PRIDE
AND
PREJUDICE

NOTES

COLES EDITORIAL BOARD

Bound to stay open

Publisher's Note

Otabind (Ota-bind). This book has been bound using the patented Otabind process. You can open this book at any page, gently run your finger down the spine, and the pages will lie flat.

ABOUT COLES NOTES

COLES NOTES have been an indispensible aid to students on five continents since 1948.

COLES NOTES are available for a wide range of individual literary works. Clear, concise explanations and insights are provided along with interesting interpretations and evaluations.

Proper use of COLES NOTES will allow the student to pay greater attention to lectures and spend less time taking notes. This will result in a broader understanding of the work being studied and will free the student for increased participation in discussions.

COLES NOTES are an invaluable aid for review and exam preparation as well as an invitation to explore different interpretive paths.

COLES NOTES are written by experts in their fields. It should be noted that any literary judgement expressed herein is just that — the judgement of one school of thought. Interpretations that diverge from, or totally disagree with any criticism may be equally valid.

COLES NOTES are designed to supplement the text and are not intended as a substitute for reading the text itself. Use of the NOTES will serve not only to clarify the work being studied, but should enhance the reader's enjoyment of the topic.

ISBN 0-7740-3331-2

© COPYRIGHT 1996 AND PUBLISHED BY
COLES PUBLISHING COMPANY
TORONTO—CANADA
PRINTED IN CANADA

Manufactured by Webcom Limited
Cover finish: Webcom's Exclusive **Duracoat**

CONTENTS

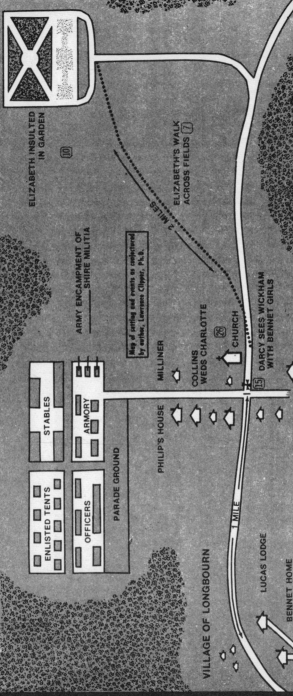

PRIDE AND PREJUDICE

HERTFORDSHIRE AREA

LONDON
24 MILES SOUTH

ELIZABETH INSULTED IN GARDEN [10]

ELIZABETH'S WALK ACROSS FIELDS [7]

ARMY ENCAMPMENT OF SHIRE MILITIA

2 MILES

STABLES

ARMORY

PARADE GROUND

ENLISTED TENTS

OFFICERS

MILLINER

COLLINS WEDS CHARLOTTE

CHURCH [26]

PHILIP'S HOUSE

Map of setting and events as conjectured by author, Lawrence Clipper, Ph.D.

DARCY SEES WICKHAM WITH BENNET GIRLS

[15]

VILLAGE OF MERYTON

1 MILE

LUCAS LODGE

BENNET HOME

ELIZABETH TALKS TO LADY CATHERINE [56]

VILLAGE OF LONGBOURN

PRIDE AND PREJUDICE

Books →	ONE	TWO	THREE
Chapters →	1 2 3 4 5 6 7 8 9 10 11 12 13 14 15 16 17 18 19 20 21 22 23	24 25 26 27 28 29 30 31 32 33 34 35 36 37 38 39 40 41 42	43 44 45 46 47 48 49 50 51 52 53 54 55 56 57 58 59 60 61

ELIZABETH and DARCY: BALL · ASSEMBLY · INSULTS ELIZABETH · WICKHAM · BALL · HUNSFORD · PROPOSAL · LETTER · RETURN · TOUR · LYDIA'S ELOPEMENT · MRS. GARDINER'S LETTER · CONFRONTS LADY CATHERINE · MARRIAGE

JANE and BINGLEY: ILL · BALL · LEAVES FOR LONDON · LONDON · HUNSFORD · INTERFERES · ARRIVAL · ARRIVES AT NETHERFIELD · PROPOSAL · MARRIAGE

LYDIA and WICKHAM: ARRIVAL · MEETS WICKHAM · MRS. FORSTER'S INVITATION · REGIMENT DEPARTS · ELOPEMENT · MARRIAGE

COLLINS and CHARLOTTE: ENTERS · PROPOSAL TO ELIZABETH · PROPOSAL TO CHARLOTTE · MARRIAGE · ELIZABETH'S VISIT

Dates →: Sept. (beg.) c. Sept. 28 · Early Oct. · Nov. 12-17 · Nov. 18 · Nov. 19 · Nov. 20 · Nov. 21 · Nov. 26 · Nov. 27 · Nov. 28 · Nov. 29 · Dec. 16 · Dec. 21-23 · Jan. 2 · March (end) · March – April · April · April or May · Day later · May (beg.) · May (2nd week) · Mid-May, June, July · July · July (end) – Aug. (beg.) · Aug. (beg.) · Aug. (end) · Sept. (beg.) · Mid Sept. · Unknown

JANE AUSTEN

DATE	AGE	BIOGRAPHICAL HIGHLIGHTS	MAJOR PUBLICATIONS
1775		BORN DECEMBER 16, AT STEVENTON, HAMPSHIRE	
1781	6	SENT TO SCHOOL AT OXFORD	
1782	7	ATTENDS SCHOOL IN SOUTHAMPTON	
1783	8	ATTENDS ABBEY SCHOOL, READING	
1795-96	20-23	COMPLETES FIRST THREE NOVELS	
			(Fragments and Juvenilia)
			Love and Friendship — 1922
			The Watsons — 1923
			Fragment of a Novel — 1925
			Plan of a Novel — 1926
1801	26	FAMILY MOVES TO BATH	
1802	27	SELLS FIRST MANUSCRIPT	
1805	30	FATHER DIES	
1808	33	MOVES TO CHAWTON	
1810	35	HEALTH BEGINS DECLINE	
1810-17	35-42	LITERARY OUTPUT WANES	(Principal Works)
1811			Sense and Sensibility
1813			Pride and Prejudice
1814			Mansfield Park
1814			Emma
1817	42	DIES, JULY 18, AT WINCHESTER	Northanger Abbey
1818			Persuasion

CONTEMPORARY EVENTS

1775	AMERICAN REVOLUTION BEGINS
1776	Declaration of Independence
1778	FRENCH TREATY WITH AMERICAN COLONIES
1783	TREATY OF PEACE ENDS AMERICAN REVOLUTION
1785	THE London Times FOUNDED
1789-93	FRENCH REVOLUTION
1792	LOUIS AND MARIE ANTOINETTE BEHEADED
1793	FRANCE AND ENGLAND AT WAR
1793	WHITNEY INVENTS COTTON GIN
1794	FALL OF ROBESPIERRE
1795-1797	REIGN OF TERROR
1796	NAPOLEON'S ITALIAN CAMPAIGN
1797	NAPOLEON INVADES AUSTRIA
1797	NELSON DESTROYS FRENCH FLEET
1798	NAPOLEON INVADES EGYPT
1799	WASHINGTON DIES
1804	NAPOLEON PROCLAIMED EMPEROR
1805	BATTLE OF TRAFALGAR
1806	HOLY ROMAN EMPIRE ENDS
1807	ABOLITION OF SLAVE TRADE
1809	LINCOLN BORN
1812	NAPOLEON'S INVASION OF RUSSIA
1813	NAPOLEON DEFEATED AT LEIPZIG
1814	TREATY OF PARIS
1815	BATTLE OF WATERLOO
1815	REORGANIZATION OF EUROPE BY CONGRESS OF VIENNA

LITERARY EVENTS:

Date	Event	Date
1775	JEFFERSON, Declaration of Independence	1776
1776	SHERIDAN, School for Scandal	1777
1778	KANT, Critique of Pure Reason	1781
1783	SCHILLER, The Robbers	1781
1785	FRENEAU, Poems	1785
1786	BURNS, Poems	1786
	GOETHE, Iphigenie	1787
	SCHILLER, Don Carlos	1787
	GOETHE, Egmont	1788
	GOETHE, Faust	1790
1795-1797	BOSWELL, Life of Johnson	1791
	PAINE, Rights of Man	1791
	PAINE, Age of Reason	1792
1797	WORDSWORTH, Lyrical Ballads	1790
1798	COLERIDGE, Lyrical Ballads	1799
1799	JOHN Q. ADAMS, Letters	1804
1804	WORDSWORTH, Prelude	1805
1805	WEBSTER, Dictionary	1806
1806	FIRST ISSUE OF Quarterly Review	1809
1807	SCOTT, Lady of the Lake	1810
1809	GRIMM, Fairy Tales	1812
1812	SCOTT, Waverley	1814
1813	MARY SHELLEY, Frankenstein	1817
1814	BYRON, Manfred	1817
1815	KEATS, Poems	1810-1820

JANE AUSTEN

PROSE

POETRY

1750   1800   1850

ENGLISH LITERATURE

SAMUEL JOHNSON 1709-1784
EDWARD GIBBON 1737-1794
LAWRENCE STERNE 1713-1768
JAMES BOSWELL 1740-1795
HENRY FIELDING 1707-1754
CHARLES LAMB 1775-1834
WM. MAKEPEACE THACKERAY 1811-1863
JOHN RUSKIN 1819-1900
CHARLES DICKENS 1812-1870
JANE AUSTEN 1775-1817
SIR WALTER SCOTT 1771-1832

THOMAS GRAY 1716-1771
LORD GEORGE BYRON 1788-1824
PERCY BYSSHE SHELLEY 1792-1822
JOHN KEATS 1795-1821
WILLIAM WORDSWORTH 1770-1850
SAMUEL TAYLOR COLERIDGE 1772-1834

WORLD LITERATURE

MONTESQUIEU 1689-1755
ROBERT BURNS 1759-1796
GOETHE 1749-1832
JAMES F. COOPER 1789-1851
EDGAR ALLAN POE 1809-1849
NATHANIEL HAWTHORNE 1804-1864
HERMAN MELVILLE 1819-1891
WALT WHITMAN 1819-1892
MARK TWAIN 1835-1910
HENRY JAMES 1843-1916

CONTEMPORARIES

ISAAC NEWTON 1642-1727
J.S. BACH 1685-1750
DENIS DIDEROT 1713-1784
MOZART 1756-1791
ROBESPIERRE 1758-1794
CHOPIN 1810-1849
ABRAHAM LINCOLN 1809-1865
KIERKEGAARD 1813-1855
FYODOR DOSTOEVSKY 1821-1881
CHARLES DARWIN 1809-1882
VAN GOGH 1853-1890
SIGMUND FREUD 1856-1939

JANE AUSTEN

Jane Austen was born at Steventon rectory on December 16, 1775. Steventon itself is a small village in the south of England, and it is in this area that she spent most of her life. There is little to say about this life except that she lived here with her family and close friends, remained unmarried, devoted herself to writing, cared for her nieces and nephews, and died relatively unknown.

As a child she was naturally dependent upon her family for entertainment, social activities, and education. What life was like at the rectory is difficult to say, but we have no reason not to imagine it as being quiet and uneventful. Her favorites, of five brothers and a sister, were Henry—who helped in the publishing of her novels—and Cassandra, with whom she corresponded all her life. She was sent for awhile to a school for young ladies at Reading, but most of her education came from within the family circle, especially from her father, who took a real interest in educating his children.

The members of the family were also responsible for educating each other. Occasionally they busied themselves with recitations, musicales, and dramatic productions, but in such an environment, the main social activities were simply walking, visiting, talking, reading, an occasional ball or dinner party, and, above all, flirtation. One witness (not necessarily to be trusted) said that Jane was the "prettiest, silliest, most affected, husband hunting butterfly" in the Steventon area. Out of this early period of her life came at least one proposal for marriage, which came to nothing.

There were occasional visits to members of the family living elsewhere in England. And, of course, there was the additional work of writing novels, often under the distracting circumstances of entertaining visitors and caring for the children.

It is best to see Jane Austen's writing career as divided into two periods, one at Steventon in the later years of the eighteenth century and a later one, the last decade of her life, at

Chawton. These two periods were separated by what was probably the most disruptive events of her life, the retirement of her aged father in 1801, and the removal of the family to Bath (and vicinity) for about nine years. For Jane her father's decision was a severe blow; it is said that she fainted away upon hearing the news. However apocryphal that story may be, her writing career came to a sudden halt, apparently because of her residence in an uncongenial urban environment.

The actual move occurred in the spring of 1801. Mother and daughters lived in Bath until Mr. Austen's death in 1805. During this brief residence in Bath—one of the most popular resort cities in Great Britain—all was not lost for Jane Austen: she refueled her imagination for the task of writing and rewriting her novels in the last years of her life. It is during these years, also, that she received a second proposal of marriage which was rejected.

After Mr. Austen's death, the family moved to Southampton. Although these were exciting years on the international scene (Napoleon made himself Emperor and planned for an invasion of England, Nelson won the battle of Trafalgar, and the war in Spain was fought), Jane's letters were characteristically devoid of any references to such world-shaking events.

In 1809, Jane Austen's exile from rural England came to an end when a brother offered Mrs. Austen a cottage at Chawton, not far from Steventon. The return to the country ended Jane's wanderings and her decade of silence. These last years were among her happiest and most productive; it is not too far-fetched to imagine her as surrounded by nieces and nephews and working at the portable desk balanced on her lap. During this period she saw the earlier three novels through the stages of publication and completed three others. Except for brief visits to London and elsewhere, she found happiness in the limited scope of village life.

The most famous event of her life occurred in 1815. Her books were then known everywhere (although she was far from popular), and they had happened to win the favor of the Prince of Wales, then Regent, and soon to be George IV. On a trip to London, Jane was invited to Carlton House, where she spoke to the librarian of the Regent. He suggested tactfully that Jane might attempt a "historical romance illustrative of the august house of Coburg." Jane—equally tactful and honest—answered that "romance" in the Sir Walter Scott vein was not her forte. She did dedicate her next novel, *Emma*, to the Prince. It appeared in 1815, receiving favorable reviews, one even written by the romantic Scott.

By 1816 Jane Austen was seriously ill, probably of cancer. In May, 1817, she went to nearby Winchester for medical advice and care. It seemed clear to everyone that the disease would prove fatal. She died in July of that year, and was buried in Winchester Cathedral.

COMPLETE BACKGROUND

Introduction

At the end of the eighteenth century, the English novel was in an ailing condition. The great masters of the novel—Fielding, Richardson, Sterne, and Smollett—were all dead, and most of the active novelists were hack writers turning out superficial imitations of the eighteenth-century masterpieces. Critics and reviewers at the time looked back to 1748 and 1749, the years when *Clarissa* and *Tom Jones* appeared, and regretted that the novel was a dead art form; for these readers, the four great eighteenth-century novelists had done all that could be done with this literary art. The only thing left for the contemporary novelist was to copy.

At this moribund stage of its history, the novel received a new impetus from the work of two great contemporaries: Jane Austen, whose first novel appeared in 1811, and Sir Walter Scott, whose epochal *Waverley* appeared in 1814. With the appearance of these two writers, the novel took on new life and quickly proved to be the dominant literary form of the Western world, a position it has not yet surrendered.

Jane Austen's career spans a very brief time. Her six novels were published within seven years, although she had been writing some years before her first publication. A measure of her artistic reputation is that at least three of these novels (*Pride and Prejudice, Mansfield Park,* and *Emma*) are frequently considered among the best novels ever written; and some readers are found to defend other novels as her best. In other words, there is a consistently high degree of artistry in her works that is perhaps unequalled by any other English novelist. While one may easily point to defective—even atrocious—novels written by Dickens, George Eliot, Conrad, James, it is difficult to find a Jane Austen novel without some worth. So excellent is her work that she has become a figure of veneration for a large body of worshippers, who are facetiously called the "Janeites."

Of Austen's six novels, that which has gained most popular favor is *Pride and Prejudice*. Although it was her second published work, it was actually the first novel she wrote (under the title, *First Impressions*). It is all the more surprising to find this novel by a young girl so satisfying as a work of art. (Some Janeites, incidentally, are resentful of the popularity of *Pride and Prejudice*, thinking it much inferior to such later works as *Emma*.) Without involving ourselves in fruitless arguments and comparisons, we need only point out that many agree *Pride and Prejudice* to be one of the most satisfying esthetic experiences a reader of English can have.

Stepping into the pages of *Pride and Prejudice* is like entering a completely different world. This is a novel that portrays a culture so unlike our own times, its characters inhabit a society so unlike ours, their problems are so different from our own, that it is extremely difficult for us to "identify" with the fictional characters portrayed. This is a quiet world quite alien to those living in the dynamic 20th century; the late 18th-century houses seem to be galaxies away from us; the wit and conversation strike us as the language of another planet. The immediate value of the novel, then, is that we become acquainted with this new world and the characters who populate it.

The alien qualities of the novel enable us perhaps to derive an even greater benefit from it: we are permitted to see the novel as a work of art. In reading any novel of the 20th century, we are too apt to lose ourselves (and our esthetic judgment) by the too easy identification of ourselves with the characters and their problems. We find it difficult to detach ourselves from the content in order to observe the form and techniques the novelist uses. In reading a Jane Austen novel, we come to appreciate more easily the techniques of the novels: her methods of characterization, her construction of plot, her subtlety of dialogue. Paradoxically, this appreciation of technique and form makes us more intensely aware of life: we come to see the people and their problems more clearly outlined, their minds and passions more plainly revealed than they are in life. The very detachment that we feel when we read a Jane Austen novel is thus an advantage in separating ourselves from our immediate situation, our daily cares, our own bias. We may even become better readers of her novels than her contemporaries were.

As someone has said, Jane Austen is "the novelist's novelist," meaning that a novelist turns to Jane Austen to see how a novel is put together. It follows necessarily that the interested reader can also turn to Jane Austen to find out how novels are written. We can thus come to understand why she has been a powerful influence on novelists from her first appearance, throughout the nineteenth century, and down to our own times. In spite of the vast differences between her world and ours, we may learn about her artistry, art in general, and the esthetic experience, from a close reading of *Pride and Prejudice*.

Jane Austen's life spanned the years 1775-1817, not a particularly long time from our point of view. Yet it might be said that her forty-one years were some of the most exciting and most revolutionary in the history of mankind. Because an artist unconsciously reflects the times in which he lives, it is not beside the point to look at the events which are a backdrop for *Pride and Prejudice*.

The Political Climate   The epoch in which Jane Austen lived was the "Age of Revolution." We are all familiar with the events which transpired in America and France in this period; in both cases, the people succeeded in throwing over the established governments—monarchies in both cases—and establishing democracies.

Most important for understanding Jane Austen—and English literature in general—is that England was relatively untouched by the violent revolutionary activity of the times. There were numerous sympathizers in England for the revolutionaries of France and the colonies (William Wordsworth and Tom Paine, to mention just two), but there was no revolution in England itself to get rid of the House of Hanover, as corrupt as it was. Why England avoided a revolution is a matter of opinion. Some historians say that memories of the bloody civil wars in the 17th century still remained. Others speak of the basically conservative "John Bull" national character, which disapproves of violence of all kinds. Economists speak of the generally favorable living conditions of the English peasant. Whatever the cause, it is true that Great Britain managed to avoid the agonies of outright rebellion experienced by France and America.

Nevertheless, Great Britain did experience a "revolution during these years which continued through the nineteenth century. This revolution—as with so many things English—occurred legally, through the continuing evolution of the British Constitution. The milestones of English history during the whole century were the great laws, like the first Reform Bill of 1832.

These changes did not occur without the accompaniment of much heat and noise, but the British did manage to avoid any wide-scale violence. The agitation and conflict took place in the courts, in the daily press, and in Parliament. And in this rather decorous manner, the English accomplished their revolution, grew into a modern industrial nation, expanded their holdings overseas, and changed their way of life.

When we look into Jane Austen's novels, we are not surprised to see that they lack the violence (insurrections, guillotines, assassinations, marching armies) which were characteristic of the European continent and America. We are more surprised, however, to find that they are without that political agitation, the strong political feelings, the revolutionary ideas which were current in her own country. The absence of these elements may be a result of another factor in her life, and in the life of the nation.

Growth of the Cities   Much of the turmoil which characterized English society and politics at the opening of the new century was a result of one factor which did not enter into the American and French revolutions, namely increasing urbanization and industrialization. Neither America nor France was to be industrialized for at least another half-century. But for the English, this is the period when those two revolutions are difficult to neglect.

Part of their story is simply a matter of the growth of population, a fact which disturbed many politicians and writers. Sheer numbers of people were changing the quality of English life. The tidiness and simplicity of traditional village life were being destroyed simply by the presence of too many people.

More important, these masses of people were moving from the villages into the larger industrial cities. For some writers (e.g. Oliver Goldsmith, in *The Deserted Village*, 1770), the fact that the villages of England were being depopulated was something

to be deplored. For other writers, the problems of the new
metropolis—the slums, hygiene, working hours—were the most
worrisome. To those of us living in the 20th century, it is easy to
visualize these early Victorian cities: the dirty slums, the black
sky, the cholera epidemics, the filthy water, the bestial level of
existence everywhere. It is a picture documented by many historians and burned into our minds by the novels of Charles
Dickens.

What surprises many readers is that although Jane Austen
lived in the years between Oliver Goldsmith and Charles Dickens, her world is neither urbanized nor industrialized. If one
were to read only her novels for information on her times, one
would never know that there were any large cities in England,
least of all that in those cities were such phenomena as factories,
cotton looms, child labor, gin palaces, slums, widespread prostitution, and the endless list of ills that beset England at the time.

Her novels remind us that throughout the century, even
down to 1914, there was another segment of English society just
as important as this new urban society: specifically, the rural
society based on the traditional hierarchy of squire, farmer, and
farm laborer. There were, as some writers remind us, many
people of all classes who were—incredible as it may seem—completely oblivious to the existence of large cities, the factory system, and the industrial masses and their attendant problems.

"A Child of the   To understand why Jane Austen's novels
18th Century"   are what they are, we must notice a few
                  salient facts. First of all, the revolutions
occurring in her time simply did not reach some of the backwater
areas in England. Steventon is in the South of England, noted for
its good farmland. The industrial revolution occurred, generally,
in the far north and northwest parts of England. The big "new"
cities—Manchester, Liverpool, Birmingham, Glasgow—were developing in the north and north-central sections of the country.
The political agitation, when it did occur, occurred in London,
far enough away in a day of bad roads and long coach rides. In
brief, Jane Austen was a country girl.

Second, Jane Austen was born between two centuries, and
is more properly seen as a child of the eighteenth century than as
a forerunner of the nineteenth century. When the century came

to an end, she was 25 years old, and most of her life was over. Also, she had formed the opinions, prejudices, attitudes, which were to stay with her to the end of her life. It is no surprise that she reflects many of the preconceptions and ideas of Edmund Burke and Samuel Johnson, rather than, say, those of John Stuart Mill and Thomas Carlyle.

Third, the Austen family atmosphere could hardly have been "revolutionary." Her father was a clergyman, her brothers were landowners, one brother was a naval officer; she came from a long line of ancestors who had given themselves to the church, farming, the military. It is only natural that such an atmosphere, such family traditions would hardly lend themselves to the creation of a revolutionary novelist, either in politics or esthetics.

Without intending to suggest that we have fully analyzed Jane Austen's soul, we may find in these facts some help in understanding the texture of her novels. Her world is neither urban nor industrial nor modern; it is usually a small world, a village or country town, in a relatively isolated rural area. The town or village is not swarming with industrial masses; her books are usually populated with two or three families and a few outsiders, these few people creating the drama. The novels are not concerned with the military, political or industrial problems faced by other parts of the country; their concerns are mainly moral or intellectual, the main concerns of the eighteenth-century writers. There is also no question of political upheaval; this is not only *not* a "revolutionary" world, it is not even a political world. That is, Jane Austen does not question any of the political premises of the eighteenth century. The people in her village are aligned in some order of rank or "degree," and some have duties of one sort, while others have responsibilities and privileges in accord with their higher rank. Behind them, presumably, is the House of Hanover, King George the Third, the Prince Regent, and the aristocracy at Westminster. Jane Austen never questions the rigid social and political system of her times. This is the traditional society of Alexander Pope, Samuel Johnson, and Edmund Burke, a system that seems outmoded to us.

The Literary Climate   Less familiar to many readers is a third revolution of the times: the revolution in literature known as "romanticism." To readers of English literature, it is clear that between 1750 and 1830, a different kind of literature began to appear. For students of literature the key date here is 1798, the date of the publication of the *Lyrical Ballads,* a collection of poetry of William Wordsworth and Samuel Taylor Coleridge.

That change of direction, or revolution, has been descri- bed by some critics as a shift from an emphasis on "reason" to an emphasis on "emotion" and the "natural." Admitting that such terms are vague at best, we can see that the literature of the time (the blank verse of Wordsworth, the sonnets of Keats, the nar- ratives of Byron) was more personal, lyrical, emotional, indivi- dualistic than the poetry of, say, Pope and Johnson. In their diction, the poets of the period hoped to rid themselves of the elegant, bookish, intellectual diction of the past (as may be observed in Pope's *Essay on Man*). In the subject matter, the literature reflected the democratic spirit of the times by using common men and women for heroes and heroines; Pope's Be- linda (in *The Rape of the Lock*) is replaced by Wordsworth's Michael and by Scott's Jeanie Deans (in *Heart of Midlothian*).

Once again, however, one sees little of this in Jane Austen. Her works show little interest in the "romantic revolution" com- ing to maturity during her lifetime. Nowhere in her letters does she mention Wordsworth, Coleridge, Shelley, Keats, Hazlitt, or Hunt. Byron she mentions only once, including him among some mundane chores, saying that she has just "read the *Corsair,* mended my petticoat, & have nothing else to do." (*Letters,* ed. Chapman, II, 379.) Her attitude toward Scott—that important force during the period—was divided; she spoke of him and his works infrequently and ambiguously. Her well-known criticism deserves repeating:

> Walter Scott has no business to write novels, espe- cially good ones.—It is not fair.—He has Fame and Profit enough as a Poet, and should not be taking the bread out of other people's mouths.—I do not like him, & do not mean to like Waverley if I can help it—but I fear I must. (*Letters,* ed. Chapman, II, 404.)

Each reader may make of this quotation what he pleases. Without a doubt, however, her loyalties are to the writers of the past. Her letters are filled with allusions to those writers, which

shows where she got the models for her style and ideas: Isaac
Bickerstaffe, Boswell, Fanny Burney, George Colman, George
Crabbe, Daniel Defoe, Henry Fielding, David Garrick, Johnson,
Milton, Pope, Richardson, Shakespeare, Sterne, Swift. These are
her models; these are her idols.

Hence, as we shall see, her own novels take on a tone, a
shape, a direction from the literature of the past. None of the
color, the sweep, the individual power, the diffuseness and pan-
oramic quality of a Scott or Byron may be found in her novels.
The writing is as controlled, disciplined, and impersonal as one
of Pope's *Moral Essays*. She attempts to achieve the universality
and classical timelessness that are the ideals of the preceding
age; she has been rightly called a "female Augustan," meaning
that her allegiance is to those writers at the beginning of the
eighteenth century, rather than to the new wave of "revolutionaries" who appeared at the beginning of the nineteenth century.
For comparisons, then, one must turn to *The Essay on Man*, not
The Prelude; to *Tom Jones* rather than to *Ivanhoe*, to *Gulliver's
Travels* rather than to *Prometheus Unbound*.

In her approach to her writing—as in her attitudes toward
society, politics, her subject matter, her view of man—Jane
Austen is a conclusion rather than a beginning. She draws to a
close an older way of writing and thinking which was dependent
on an older society long since disappeared. Yet in saying this we
must quickly add that she is not "outmoded" or "irrelevant" to
our times. Paradoxically, her "outmoded" novels seem to be more
applicable to our lives than the daring deeds of Walter Scott's
Ivanhoe or the gloomy melancholy of Lord Byron's *Corsair*. Why
this strange fact is so will emerge from our discussion.

CAPSULE SUMMARY

The arrival of a new neighbor, wealthy Mr. Bingley, promises to solve a problem for the Bennet family: they see him as an eligible bachelor for one of their five marriageable daughters. Their hopes are borne out when he is attracted to the eldest daughter, Jane. The next oldest, Elizabeth, however, takes an instant dislike to Bingley's friend, Fitzwilliam Darcy, who appears to be a proud, supercilious man. While Jane's affair progresses, Elizabeth is courted by a Mr. Collins, an unlikeable churchman who is a cousin of Mr. Bennet's and the legal heir to the small Bennet estate. When Elizabeth refuses his proposal, Collins turns to her best friend, Charlotte Lucas, who surprises everyone by accepting; she has found a comfortable, secure life at the cost of marrying an obsequious fool.

Jane's chances of winning Bingley are diminished when he leaves for London. His sister Caroline and Darcy contrive to keep him there in order to prevent any further progress of this affair with Jane, who is not in Bingley's social class. Elizabeth finds another reason for disliking Darcy when she hears from a fop named Wickham, who has flattered her shamefully, that Darcy had ruined his prospects years before.

On a visit to Collins' parsonage, Elizabeth meets Darcy again, and is astonished when he proposes. She refuses and berates him for his treatment of Jane and Wickham. He explains in a letter that he had not realized the depth of Jane's affection for Bingley, hence had not seen the separation as a calamity. As for Wickham, that young man is really a scoundrel who had attempted to seduce Darcy's sister and to get her money. Elizabeth begins to suspect that she had misjudged Darcy; her doubt is reinforced when she meets him again at his estate and finds him to be a gracious host who is virtually worshipped by his employees.

Their reconciliation is jeopardized, however, by the sudden elopement of Wickham and Lydia, the youngest Bennet girl. The Bennets are in a position where they must pay Wickham to marry their daughter. Surprisingly, however, the sum Wickham demands is relatively small. It is soon revealed that Darcy has paid an additional amount to the scoundrel.

Elizabeth realizes from this that Darcy is in love with her. Shortly, Bingley arrives at the village again to renew his acquaintance with Jane. Darcy and Elizabeth apologize to each other for their initial pride and prejudice. And, in spite of protests from their families, Bingley and Darcy marry Jane and Elizabeth and take them off to comfortable futures.

COMPREHENSIVE SUMMARY

Note on Chapter numbers:
Pride and Prejudice was originaly published in three volumes, the first having 23 chapters, the second and third having 19 chapters each. Some modern editions retain this method of numbering, while other editions number the chapters consecutively from 1 to 61. For the convenience of those who may have either edition, this guide supplies numbers for both types.

Chapter 1 (I, 1)   Mr. and Mrs. Bennet discuss the recent rental of a nearby estate, Netherfield Park, by a Mr. Bingley. The news gladdens the heart of Mrs. Bennet, who has five daughters to marry off; she urges Mr. Bennet to make a proper social call on the new neighbor. He teases his wife, saying that he will leave such formalities to her; of course, he secretly plans to make the visit.

COMMENTARY: This is an important chapter, for the novelist quickly establishes the main situation: the arrival of Bingley and the need to marry off the Bennet girls. Like many of her other novels, this shows Jane Austen's characteristic subject matter: the arrival of a marriageable young man in a village and the stratagems of the women to trap him. As many critics point out, underneath the sheen and culture of Jane Austen's world, there is something primeval, basic, predatory: it is a world where men are trapped, where women must find mates in order to survive. It is a world in which the economic facts of life are not to be denied.

This dark side of Jane Austen's thinking is pointed up immediately by the first sentence of the book, surely one of the finest sentences in the English language. It is a complex sentence which embodies the subject matter and ironic tone of the whole novel. On the surface, it states a simple fact: many people *do assume* that a young man with money must want a wife. Beneath this, however, is the ironic thought that the young man may actually be the hunted rather than the hunter; it is quite likely that the women in the area must be in want of such a husband. And yet, beneath this irony is the psychological conclusion that any young man must, quite normally, wish to be married. The sentence is a perfect example of the complexity of Jane Austen's prose style, and gives some indication of the care one must take in reading her.

Notice that in the next paragraph the young man is even called the "rightful property" of some young lady. There the direction of the novel is more plainly marked out: Bingley is already being measured and considered by the ladies present. The rest of the novel will develop the subject indicated by these two sentences: it will be a book about the complex subject of men hunting for wives, and ladies hunting for husbands, and all the ironies involved in such pursuits.

The chapter also gives us the characters of two important people: the elder Bennets. Mrs. Bennet is silly and shallow, yet we approve of her concern for her children. Mr. Bennet is more complex: he is sensible, has a sense of perspective, and can be disinterested about the things which upset his wife. Yet there is a touch of irresponsibility in this detachment from things which, in spite of their inanity, are serious matters for concern. What will happen to his daughters when he dies?

Clearly they are a mismatched pair, our first example of a bad marriage. The fact that Mrs. Bennet approves of Lydia's "good humor" and Jane's "handsomeness" while Mr. Bennet prefers his daughter Elizabeth is symptomatic of their incompatibility.

Chapter 2 (I, 2)   Mrs. Bennet is in a state of despair: unless her husband makes the formal call on Mr. Bingley, there is little hope (under the social code) that her daughters can meet him. In the family circle, she is alternately excited, accusatory, self-pitying; she worries especially that some other mother with an eligible daughter will win the race. Mr. Bennet, unable to endure her irritability, informs her that he has made the formal call to Netherfield Park. The mother and daughters collapse ecstatically into a state of relief and anticipation.

COMMENTARY: Mr. and Mrs. Bennet are revealed more clearly to us. She seems utterly unequal to the problem facing her; restricted by the rigid code of the period, she can do nothing to advance the fortunes of her daughters, who seem to be her main responsibility. Frustrated by these rules, she vents her feelings on petty annoyances, such as Kitty's coughing.

Mr. Bennet seems entirely capable and reasonable about the family affairs. Still, there is something cold and unpleasant about him. At the least, he has played a nasty joke, by keeping his women in a state of agonized suspense all day. We can also conclude that he is thoroughly unhappy with his present situation; he is intellectually superior to his wife and most of his daughters, and quite contemptuous of their petty concerns. He is capable of cutting sarcasm too, as when he comments on Mary's "deep reflection" and Kitty's coughing. Nevertheless, he has acted, and a small step has been made to bring the major characters together.

Chapter 3 (I, 3) The Bennets come to know Mr. Bingley in a series of meetings as formal as a minuet. Within a fortnight, a large ball is held; Mr. Bingley brings with him two sisters, one brother-in-law, and a friend, Mr. Darcy. The ball is a decided success; Mrs. Bennet's hopes soar when Mr. Bingley takes an interest in Jane. The only blot on the evening is Mr. Darcy, who remains aloof from the predatory females and dances only with Miss Bingley. Elizabeth Bennet is half amused when she overhears Darcy say that Jane is "the only handsome girl in the room" and that Elizabeth herself is "not handsome enough to tempt me." Mrs. Bennet returns home to bore her husband with news of the triumph.

COMMENTARY: The two main characters in the novel begin to emerge, and the plot begins on an unpromising note. Darcy is made unsympathetic both to the other characters and to the reader. We are informed that Darcy "was discovered to be proud"; we see him refusing to be introduced to anyone; and his insulting comments show him to be contemptuous of those beneath him. Notice, however, that Jane Austen is dropping contradictory clues in the dialogue. Is not Darcy somewhat justified in not wishing to dance with strangers? And is not Mrs. Bennet's disapproval ("I quite detest the man.") possibly meant to arouse in the reader just the opposite response, since we are already aware that she is quite shallow?

The other important character we meet, although only briefly, is Elizabeth Bennet, the heroine. We see first of all that she is not the heroine of a romantic novel. Far from being unbelievably beautiful and infinitely desirable to the hero, she is a wallflower! Our interest in her is immediately stimulated by the amusement she finds in Darcy's insult: she is even willing to tell a funny story on herself and on a point which finds women most sensitive—her beauty. She seems to be original, likeable, even eccentric.

Notice in the future, however, that Elizabeth does not recover from this insult, for she, too, is a proud person. Many readers have assumed that the title of the novel refers specifically to Darcy's "pride" and Elizabeth's "prejudice," and that the novel is about his pride and her prejudice being overcome and eventually defeated. This is an oversimplification of Jane Austen's purposes. One might, indeed, argue that Darcy is without any "pride," if by "pride" we mean selfishness or self-interest. Certainly Elizabeth is as proud as he is. Darcy's pride disappears quite early in the book (by Chapter 6 he is humbling himself in order to win her affection!). Her prejudice continues throughout much of the book, and that prejudice is largely a result of her wounded pride. It is certainly an error to see either vice—pride or prejudice—as belonging exclusively to either the hero or heroine. Jane Austen's characters are more complex than that. Elizabeth is proud of her understanding, her intellect, her superior personality, and she quickly is prejudiced against a man who fails to recognize these immediately; Darcy is proud of his social position and prejudiced against the rural people he meets in the first chapters of the book. Both hero and heroine will be purified of these errors.

Chapter 4 (I, 4)   Alone, Jane and Elizabeth discuss the ball and
                     Mr. Bingley. Jane's self-depreciation leads
Elizabeth to comment on her sister's personality: she finds parti-

cularly dangerous Jane's willingness to overlook the faults of others, for example, the Bingley sisters. The novelist ends the chapter with the background of the Bingley family and a comparison of Mr. Bingley and Darcy.

COMMENTARY: This chapter is primarily engaged in developing two sets of contrasts: Elizabeth versus Jane, and Mr. Bingley versus Darcy. It is therefore providing the reader with his first extensive look at the four major figures who will engage his attention for the rest of the book.

The first contrast is achieved largely through dialogue. We see that Jane is a pleasant, rather naive young girl who thinks the whole world is as decent and simple as she is. Her intelligence has no depths, as she reveals in her enumeration of Bingley's virtues: "He is sensible, good-humored, lively . . . has happy manners; so much ease with such perfect good breeding!" Elizabeth adds sarcastically that he is also "handsome." Elizabeth Bennet is revealed to be realistic, intelligent, and frank to the point of bad manners. She is candid "without ostentation or design," her frankness arising out of the fear that her sister may be hurt. Notice that she has immediately penetrated to an understanding of the Bingley family.

The second set of contrasts is not a result of dialogue but of Jane Austen's overt discussion of the two young men, Darcy and Bingley. Bingley is revealed to be like Jane: his quick renting of Netherfield shows a similar, easy impressionability. Darcy, we are told, is superior in intelligence, but his aloof manners tend to make him unpopular. He is parallel to Elizabeth in his frankness and clearsightedness; he is unimpressed by the considerations which impress other men.

The pattern of the two couples is established quickly, partly through dialogue, partly through explicit statement. As for plot, the only thing we can be certain of at this point is Jane's admiration of Bingley.

Chapter 5 (I, 5)   Mrs. Bennet and her daughters visit their neighbors, Mrs. Lucas and her daughters. (Sir

William Lucas, once a businessman, has retired to his estate in Meryton.) The ladies are aglow over the ball, especially over Jane's personal triumph: her two dances with Mr. Bingley. The conversation shifts to the insulting Mr. Darcy and his comments on Elizabeth's appearance.

COMMENTARY: This chapter accomplishes two things. First, Darcy's pride becomes a matter of serious discussion, and through it the revelation of prejudice against him is made. The prejudice is clear: the others condemn him, although they know nothing about his true character.

The second function of the chapter is to add more clues to warn the reader against the false information being given. For example, there is a brief argument over whether Darcy actually spoke to Mrs. Long. If he did, as Jane seems sure, can we be certain his character is bad? Furthermore, as Charlotte Lucas says, Darcy "has a right to be proud," in his family, his upbringing, his fortune, and his appearance, he is certainly a young man to be envied. To this argument, even Elizabeth gives assent. The lecture on pride given by Mary is a nonsensical collection of platitudes that have no bearing on his personality. The reader's mind should at this point be in a state of suspense about Darcy's character.

Chapter 6 (I, 6) Elizabeth and Charlotte Lucas discuss the growing attraction between Bingley and Jane. Elizabeth is happy that Jane makes no great display of her affection, but Charlotte urges that Jane should make use of every moment she has with Bingley. Elizabeth says that Jane does not yet know Bingley very well; Charlotte replies that there is time enough to get to know each other *after* the wedding. Elizabeth ends the conversation by saying, ". . . you would never act in this way yourself."

COMMENTARY: Charlotte's attitude and her abstract discussion of marriage are indications of her own uncertainties and preparations for her actions later in the book. Since she is without a husband, she necessarily sees marriage as a matter of tactics and maneuvering. She is cynical about marriage itself: if it is simply a matter of baiting a trap, one should not care too much about what one catches.

This attitude contrasts nicely with Elizabeth Bennet's philosophy: she will marry Darcy only after they have learned much about each other and themselves.

Meanwhile—we are surprised to hear—Darcy has discovered that Elizabeth is more attractive than he first thought her. He begins to look at her, listen to her, desire her company; at a dinner party, he is impressed by her independent spirit. She is unaware of the attraction and sees no outward change in Darcy.

COMMENTARY: Darcy's original prejudice against Elizabeth begins to dissolve, while hers remains intact, probably because of his refusal to dance with her at the first ball. The chapter is important in that the gap between the hero and heroine begins to shrink, largely from Darcy's initiative. Some critics have complained that Darcy's change of heart is not credible, especially since we are asked to believe in this brief paragraph that his coldness toward Elizabeth is now dissipated. Actually, Darcy's change of attitude is not so hard to believe. Clearly he is interested in her because she is unlike all the other women he has encountered so far in his life; most of these have been shallow, selfish, and predatory. The force of her intellect and her independent personality is something new in his experience.

The chapter ends with a conversation between Darcy and Miss Caroline Bingley. She discovers his interest in Elizabeth and chides him for it.

COMMENTARY: Elizabeth's nemesis appears in the form of Caroline Bingley, one of the least attractive figures of English literature. Her presence in these early scenes is an important element in the novel: she is an example of the kind of woman Darcy has known so far in his life— shallow, selfish, and predatory. Throughout the book she functions as a "foil" to Elizabeth, a strong contrast by which Darcy can measure the excellence of the woman he loves. Caroline is constantly damaging her own cause by attempting to gain Darcy's affection; the more she pursues, the more he flees. And he runs into the arms of Elizabeth.

Chapter 7 (I, 7)   The first paragraph discusses the economic facts of life for the five Bennet daughters. Their father's estate, Longbourn, is "entailed" upon the nearest male relative. That is, no female can inherit the estate; this means that husbands must be found to provide for the girls after Mr. Bennet's death.

COMMENTARY: This innocuous paragraph reveals the harsh economic realities underlying the veneer of English culture at this time. In the late 18th and early 19th centuries, the typical English woman had no economic or legal standing in society. Unable to make a living for herself, she was supported by the males in her family until some other male volunteered to provide for her maintenance through matrimony. Her economic position was made more unstable since she was legally forbidden from inheriting the family estate. This is the situation the Bennet girls find themselves in. Without any formal education, without any training that might have prepared them for a profession or occupation, and prevented by the "entail" from inheriting Longbourn, they are now preoccupied with thoughts of capturing a husband. (See also *Critical Analysis.*)

An army regiment is now stationed in the nearby village of Meryton, much to the delight of Kitty and Lydia, the man-hungry youngest daughters. On the pretext of visiting the Philips family, relatives in Meryton, they have been visiting the village frequently. This gives rise to a discussion by Mr. and Mrs. Bennet over the dangers of these flirtations.

COMMENTARY: Characteristically, this is the extent of Jane Austen's comment on the international troubles in her lifetime: the army provides husbands for her heroines. The argument between Mr. and Mrs. Bennet reveals their personalties: Mrs. Bennet's approval of her daughters' flirtations shows how shallow her values are. Especially damning is her admission that she can still be excited by a uniform. Mr. Bennet does not come off completely acquitted: he may disapprove of the flirtations, but he seems helpless, or too confused, to provide the strong authority that is needed.

Jane receives a surprise invitation to Netherfield Park for dinner. The Bennets—and especially Mrs. Bennet—are overjoyed. When the weather turns bad, Mrs. Bennet is in ecstasy, seeing a real possibility that Jane may be invited to stay overnight. Jane goes to Netherfield, predictably catches cold, and is asked to remain there for some time. Elizabeth walks in the rain and mud to take care of her sister; she arrives muddy and bedraggled, much to the delight of Caroline Bingley.

COMMENTARY: The continued scheming of the English female is made obvious. As Mr. Bennet says sarcastically, "If Jane should die, it would be a comfort to know that it was all in pursuit of Mr. Bingley." The "fortuitous" event does prepare a wide path for the Bennet sisters, since it throws them in close proximity to the eligible bachelors. As the chapter closes, however, Elizabeth has apparently disgraced herself in Darcy's eyes; he seems to be embarrassed by her condition after her walk. Once again, however, appearances are deceiving: although it is clear the Bingley sisters are amused, Darcy sees something noble in Elizabeth's self-sacrifice.

Chapter 8 (I; 8)   Elizabeth has her clothes sent to Netherfield and settles into a routine of caring for Jane. She is the subject of much ridicule by the Bingley sisters, but Mr. Bingley and—suprisingly—Mr. Darcy defend Elizabeth's gesture. The Bingley sisters' continued sarcasm now is directed against the Bennet family, who show their inferior social rank by having been in "trade." The gentlemen are unimpressed by this criticism as well.

COMMENTARY: Miss Bingley is clearly aiming to discredit Elizabeth in the eyes of Darcy. He wins the reader's sympathy by resisting her snobbish arguments, showing himself as a man of good sense.

Jane is still sick. One evening Elizabeth comes downstairs to find the others playing cards; she refuses to join them, saying that she prefers to read a book. A long discussion ensues on the qualities of a mature woman, during which Darcy shows a clear preference for thoughtful, intelligent women like Elizabeth. Miss Bingely again is thrown into confusion.

During this chapter the gap between Darcy and Elizabeth is further diminished: she has proven herself by the reckless, but unselfish, gesture of walking across the country to help her sister. Her preference for reading rather than card-playing and embroidery makes her more attractive to Darcy than she was. The two may have started on the wrong foot, but the reader at least can perceive that Darcy and Elizabeth are suited for each other, though Darcy is not quite prepared to go so far, and Elizabeth has not yet begun, at least consciously, to depart from her original dislike of Darcy. Darcy continues to win the reader's sympathy by his resistance to Miss Bingley's flattery and sarcasm.

Chapter 9 (I, 9)   Mrs. Bennet arrives to examine Jane; she finds her much improved, but not wishing to extricate the girl from this ideal confinement, she asserts that she is sicker than she really is. Mr. Bingley seems contented with the diagnosis, happy that Jane must stay on at Netherfield. Once the decision is agreed upon, the company exchange views on a number of small matters. During the conversation Mrs. Bennet succeeds in making a fool of herself: she coyly insults Darcy, argues the virtues of country living, gossips about Charlotte Lucas, and boasts endlessly about Jane. Lydia does not help matters by her chatter about dancing. Somehow Elizabeth survives the embarrassment of her mother's visit, and when Mrs. Bennet departs she retreats upstairs. Miss Bingley uses the visit for further insulting remarks about the Bennet family.

COMMENTARY: This is certainly Mrs. Bennet's chapter. Here we see the main facets of her personality neatly displayed: her shallowness in the affairs of the world, her transparent ambitions for her daughters, a streak of cruelty, and obtuseness in reading character. Her personality throws a light on the personalities of Elizabeth (who turns out to be long-suffering and tolerant) and Darcy, who is embarrassed for Mrs. Bennet, yet sympathetic toward Elizabeth. Above all, Darcy can see that a bad family has not succeeded in ruining Elizabeth's character; she is all the more a marvel for having turned out well.

Chapter·10 (I, 10)   A humorous scene occurs in which Darcy is
                        writing a letter to his sister while Miss Bing-
ley flatters him shamefully. Darcy pointedly ignores her compliments and virtually insults her for her troubles.

COMMENTARY: The contrast between two ways of writing is
                 meant to be read as a contrast of two kinds of
personality. Darcy writes carefully, slowly, while Bingley,
it is said, writes rapidly, without thought. There is an implicit compliment, in this society, in saying that someone
can do things without thought, with a rapidity; somehow
this is more admirable than to be one of those who act
slowly and with deliberation. This is *not* the view held by
Darcy, and *not* the view held by Jane Austen. Bingley
admits that his letters' end in blots, and "convey no ideas
at all." Darcy is the man of thought, of reason; he will get
things done, and his life will be more stable.

Elizabeth becomes aware of Darcy's eyes during the musi-
cal recital. She imagines that he disapproves of her, since she is
totally unaware of his growing interest in her. She rejects his
invitation to dance on the assumption that he is somehow insulting her.

COMMENTARY: Elizabeth's prejudice continues to work on her.
                 Like many of Jane Austen's heroines, she is blind
at the beginning of the novel and must progress through
experience and learning to a point where she is deserving
of marriage. Darcy, in his turn, is tolerant of her coolness,
realizing the unsatisfactory impression he must have made
on this fascinating and intelligent woman. Indeed, her
reticence impresses him favorably, especially when contrasted with the advances made by Caroline Bingley, who
seems to share Charlotte's ideas of how to trap a man.
Such plans may work with a Collins or a Bingley, but
clearly Darcy is a different kind of man.

Miss Bingley's campaign to discredit Elizabeth (and pave
the way for herself) continues in her private talks with Darcy.
He remains unconvinced. In the garden one day he is strongly
offended by a deliberate affront directed against Elizabeth by
Caroline.

Miss Bingley's character grows more detestable the closer Darcy comes to Elizabeth. She unwittingly helps to drive Darcy into Elizabeth's arms.

Chapter 11 (I, 11) Jane emerges from her sick room, well enough to mingle in society. After dinner, the group at Netherfield busy themselves with reading, singing, and conversation. Miss Bingley tries in vain to capture Darcy's attention. Elizabeth and Darcy talk about vices in general, and the shortcomings of Darcy's personality.

COMMENTARY: The discussion between Darcy and Elizabeth gives us an insight into one human quality which Jane Austen approves of: the understanding, or reason, which must be in control of one's whims, follies, emotions. Hence, the relevance of Darcy's analysis of Elizabeth: her main fault or weakness is "wilfully to misunderstand" everybody, including Darcy. Because of her prejudice, she is farther from the truth than Darcy, who has already come to admire her; her analysis of his main weakness—that he has "a propensity to hate everybody"—shows how wrong she is.

Chapter 12 (I, 12) Jane is now thoroughly recovered. Mrs. Bennet attempts to prolong her stay for a few more days, but Elizabeth is determined to leave Netherfield. Everyone except Bingley seems happy to see them leave; even Darcy now wishes to be rid of Elizabeth's presence, feeling that her appeal has grown dangerously strong. The girls return to Longbourn, much to the disappointment of Mrs. Bennet. Mr. Bennet welcomes them, however, having suffered from the senseless discussions of the Meryton regiment ever since their departure.

COMMENTARY: This chapter ends one small cycle of the book's movement: the first stage in the growth of the two love affairs. Jane and Bingley are well on their way to solidifying their union, if events (and Mrs. Bennet) will only permit; they have found each other highly congenial. Darcy, perhaps realizing that his affair is moving too rapidly, is happy to have a temporary pause. He is a person who approves of slowness, thought, concentration, deliberation—in his handwriting and in his love affairs; circumstances have been too pat, too contrived perhaps, to satisfy him. He believes that he needs time to recover, ponder, analyze his relationship with Elizabeth; hence he welcomes the separation from the woman he loves (or is growing to love), a period when emotion may be "recollected in tranquility." He is no ardent lover, no "romantic" driven by a mad, delirious passion. In Jane Austen's view, true love and a good marriage must be based on time, thought, and calm deliberation.

Chapter 13 (I, 13)   Mr. Bennet informs his family that they soon will receive a visit from his cousin, Mr. William Collins, the male relative who will some day inherit the estate. Mrs. Bennet is outraged at the very thought of a visit from this stranger, the representative of an unjust system which makes her daughters' future so uncertain. Collins is the rector at Hunsford Parsonage in Kent, Hunsford being part of Rosings, the estate of Lady Catherine de Bourgh. His letter reveals Collins to be pompous, foolish, utterly obsequious to Lady Catherine.

COMMENTARY: The letter is one example of Jane Austen's lifelong interest in writing style; her first attempts at writing were parodies of the styles of popular novelists. For her, as for the French, the style is the man: that is, a man reveals himself by how he speaks and writes. Elizabeth Bennet quickly determines from the letter that the man is "very pompous . . . a mixture of servility and self-importance." This is exactly what Mr. Collins proves to be. Throughout the book he and other characters reveal the truth about themselves by the way they talk and write.

Mr. Collins arrives, grave, stately, formal. The tension in the air which arises from his position as the legal heir is somewhat diminished by the obsequious manner he adopts in talking to Mrs. Bennet.

COMMENTARY: The style of the letter proves to be an accurate indication of the man. Mr. Collins is one of the most distasteful characters in the English novel, yet in a harmless way: he is young, but shows the pomposity of an old man; he is sugary, and lacks any real strength of character. His compliments to the Bennet girls are hints to the wary reader of his real purpose for visiting.

Chapter 14 (I, 14)   Mr. Collins expounds at great length the virtues of Lady Catherine de Bourgh, the grande dame whom he serves as rector. He informs everyone that Lady Catherine has been "kind" enough on several occasions to interfere with his life: most recently she has advised him strongly to get married. Mr. Bennet and Elizabeth take great delight in watching Mr. Collins reveal what an ass he is. He prides himself, for example, on his ability to flatter Lady Catherine. Asked to read to the family after dinner, he haughtily rejects a novel given to him and chooses a book of sermons. The reader can even sympathize with Lydia, who is utterly crushed by the boredom of the scene.

COMMENTARY: Mr. Collins is revealed to be an unlikeable toady who is capable only of conventional thinking and the most absurd ambitions. He is amenable to the debasing situation at Hunsford, where he is at the mercy of Lady Catherine. He is a victim of stale thought, conventional platitudes, and stock responses; he is false, hypocritical, and pretentious. Thus he makes a perfect foil for the sensible people, like Mr. Bennet and Elizabeth. And it is significant that Mrs. Bennet quickly accepts him as a fine fellow.

In this chapter we are given an indirect view of Lady Catherine de Bourgh, an unpleasant woman who surrounds herself with oafs like Collins.

Chapter 15 (I, 15)   Jane Austen informs us directly that Mr. Collins' character is a "mixture of pride and obsequiousness, self-importance and humility." As we suspect, he is at Longbourn to win one of the Bennet girls as a wife. At first he is intent on having Jane, but Mrs. Bennet quickly hints that Jane has hopes elsewhere. It is not difficult for Mr. Collins to shift his attentions to Elizabeth.

COMMENTARY: As a part of the plot, the sequence of Collins' wooing of the Bennet sisters is a dead-end, in that nothing comes of it. However, the sequence is very important as another part of Jane Austen's discussion of marriage. She shows that Collins is easily able to shift his attention from one girl to another; this is one way of finding a wife quickly, but it is hardly a sound foundation for a marriage. Lady Catherine has let it be known that any self-respecting clergyman is a married man, and Collins is eagerly seeking a wife who can help him create this "image." We can see that he has no feeling for either Jane or Elizabeth, nor does he know much about them. It is clear that Jane Austen deplores such an approach toward marriage, which lacks any mutual respect or affection. They are marriages of convenience, designed less for the happiness of the individuals involved than for some ulterior purpose.

Mr. Collins accompanies the Bennet girls on a walk to Meryton. In town they meet a friend, Mr. Denny, who introduces them to a George Wickham; Wickham is in Meryton waiting for a commission in the regiment. Coincidentally, at this moment, Bingley and Darcy ride into town and see the group standing on the street talking. Elizabeth observes that Wickham and Darcy know each other, that they are both embarrassed, even upset, by this chance meeting. She wonders what it can mean. The Bennet girls and Collins visit the Philipses and are invited to dinner the following day.

COMMENTARY: A second alien element is injected into the life of the Bennet family. Collins has already entered the scene and can disrupt the calm by proposing to one of the girls. Now Wickham enters; playing only a minor role in this chapter, he will eventually prove to be even more disruptive than Collins.

Chapter 16 (I, 16)   The scene is the supper party at the Philipses. By chance, Elizabeth is thrown into the company of Wickham. A long conversation ensues, during which Wickham amazes Elizabeth with a detailed account of his former dealings with Darcy. Wickham had been brought up at Pemberley, the Darcy family estate; there his father had been a kind of supervisor for the Darcy property, and he himself had been a boyhood friend of Fitzwilliam Darcy. The elder Wickham had been so competent that Darcy's father had promised to take care of his son; according to Wickham, he had been promised a career in the church and a "living" (clerical position) at Pemberley. After his father's death, the present Mr. Darcy (a jealous and vengeful person) had turned Wickham off the estate and failed to keep his father's promises. Infatuated by Wickham's appearance and flattered by his having chosen her to relate his story to, Elizabeth is completely taken in; she is certain that Darcy is a contemptible, implacable enemy. She also hears from Wickham that Lady Catherine de Bourgh is Darcy's aunt; hence two people she dislikes are linked in her mind together.

COMMENTARY: This long and important chapter creates another barrier between Darcy and Elizabeth. Wickham's story succeeds in further alienating the two major characters, decreasing the possibility of reconciliation.

Wickham's character is presented fully through his conversation. He is a handsome, confident, but shallow young man. To even a casual reader he appears to be either (a) a liar—if his story turns out to be false, or (b) bad-mannered and malevolent, even if he is telling the truth. Who but a malicious person would tell such a story to a total stranger, as Wickham has done?

Elizabeth's character is illuminated, too, by the conversation. Here she is clearly a victim of her prejudice against Darcy, for she is completely deceived by Wickham's story. Her gullibility is partly a result of the setting: she is flattered that Wickham has chosen her as a confidante, rather than the more attractive girls in the room. He contrasts nicely with Darcy, who had ignored her on an earlier social occasion. For all of her intelligence, she is being duped by Wickham; she fails to see that anyone who tells such a story—even if true—cannot be deserving of her trust. In Jane Austen's view, Elizabeth has committed a gross error: she has been taken in by Wickham's "appearance" rather than attempting to *know* the "reality" of his situation. She will have to do penance by growing to knowledge and self-awareness through the rest of the novel.

Note Jane Austen's characteristic use of a minor incident to underline a major one: Elizabeth is as prepared to dislike Lady Catherine (though she has never seen her) as she is to accept unconfirmed testimony against Darcy.

Chapter 17 (I, 17)   Speaking to Jane about Wickham's story, Elizabeth reveals the extent to which she has been deceived: "I can much more easily believe Mr. Bingley's being imposed on (by Darcy) than that Mr. Wickham should invent such a history of himself as he gave me last night."

COMMENTARY: Elizabeth's statement that "Besides, there was truth in his look" reveals precisely the extent of her delusion. Jane Austen is showing how appearances are undependable, and how the real truth about people lies underneath, to be discovered only after long experience and analysis.

The Bennet girls receive an invitation to the long-awaited ball at Netherfield, to be held on the following Tuesday. Elizabeth looks forward to dancing with Wickham, a sign that she is enchanted by this scoundrel. Her reveries are interrupted by Mr. Collins, who asks her for the first two dances, Suddenly she realizes in horror that he intends to propose to her.

COMMENTARY: Elizabeth's continuing ignorance about Wickham's character is counterpointed with her discovery of Collins' motives. There are indications that Elizabeth is slightly in love with Wickham, the man who has flattered her with attentions.

Chapter 18 (I, 18)   It is the night of the ball at Netherfield. Elizabeth's dreams of dancing with Wickham end when she discovers that he will not attend; he has gone to town on business, ostensibly, but no one doubts that the real reason is "to avoid a certain gentleman here." Elizabeth's prejudice against Darcy deepens.

The evening which had promised to be a gay affair turns out to be one disaster after another. Her dances with Collins are an agony. A brief discussion of the Wickham affair with Darcy leaves Elizabeth unsatisfied. Sir William Lucas interrupts their conversation with an embarrassing comment on the future happiness of Bingley and Jane. Miss Bingley defends Darcy and gossips maliciously about Wickham's personality.

Worse follows. Mr. Collins—a relative of the Bennet family—introduces himself to Darcy—an offense against the social

code. Darcy retreats coldly from the presence of this social upstart who boasts of being in the retinue of Darcy's relative, Lady
Catherine. At supper Mrs. Bennet talks grandly about the coming
alliance between the Bingleys and the Bennets, as though the
nuptials of the young couple are a foregone conclusion. Elizabeth
notices uneasily that Darcy is listening with "steady gravity."
Mary ends the catastrophic evening with an overlong display of
her singing.

COMMENTARY: "To Elizabeth it appeared that had her family
made an agreement to expose themselves as much
as they could during the evening, it would have been impossible for them to play their parts with more spirit or
finer success." The evening succeeds in driving Elizabeth
and Darcy further apart. Elizabeth's prejudice is unaba-
ted; she says of Darcy and Wickham, "I shall venture still
to think of both gentlemen as I did before." Ironically,
her sympathy for Wickham is increased by the fact that
her enemy, Caroline Bingley, defends Darcy so energetically. Worst of all, Darcy is suddenly made aware of the
general expectation that Bingley will marry Jane Bennet.
To a friend like Darcy, Bingley seems surrounded by
scheming social-climbers. Darcy's character is deeply offended by the rapidity of events and disturbed by Bingley's seeming unawareness of the plots being hatched
around him. These factors, supported perhaps by his attempt to resist the attraction he feels for Elizabeth, will
force him to act to prevent the marriage.

The party breaks up. Darcy seems "disengaged," and does
not speak to Elizabeth. Bingley informs everyone that he is going
to London for a short visit. Mrs. Bennet returns to Longbourn,
optimistic about the marriage of Jane to Bingley, and the marriage of Elizabeth ("the least dear to her of all her children") to
Mr. Collins.

COMMENTARY: The evening seems to have made an irreparable
shambles of the situation. Mrs. Bennet's utter
stupidity is revealed nowhere so clearly as at the end of
this chapter where her hopes are even higher than before
of a satisfactory conclusion to her arrangements. She
misses entirely the storm warnings of the evening. Darcy's
silence and his remoteness from Elizabeth are clear signs

that they are farther apart than ever. Bingley's announced trip to London is more bad news: given his malleable personality (see I, 10) and the malicious character of Miss Bingley, the reader may anticipate a cooling of the affair with Jane.

Chapter 19 (I, 19) The following morning Elizabeth must meet another crisis. Mr. Collins, receiving the approval of Mrs. Bennet, proposes to Elizabeth. Mechanically and portentously he announces the reasons for the proposal. First, it is right for clergymen to marry. Second, it will make him happy. Third, he has been urged to do so by Lady Catherine de Bourgh; and fourth, he has chosen a prospective bride from among the Bennet sisters in order to ease their minds about the estate. Characteristically, he spends as much time on Lady Catherine and abstract arguments as he does on the female he is proposing to. When Elizabeth refuses the proposal, Mr. Collins' ego is too inflated to recognize the insult: he attributes her negative response to the "romantic" notions of young girls, who like to turn down proposals at least once and sustain the suspense. Elizabeth assures him that her decision is one made by a "rational creature;" Collins coyly promises to ask again.

COMMENTARY: Jane Austen's satire of Collins' character is expanded: we now see him as an abject puppet of Lady Catherine, unable to think for himself even in personal matters.

On the other hand, some of the true worth of Elizabeth Bennet emerges in this chapter. Jane Austen leaves implicit the important economic factors behind Elizabeth's rejection of Collins: she is a young girl without any livelihood, any profession, and (especially after the last chapter) few hopes of winning Darcy (at this point, of course, she does not believe that she wants him). Collins' offer is attractive in many ways: there is the promise of a comfortable life, not only for herself, but for her family. Elizabeth's rejection, then, is an act of courage and honesty, the act of a "rational creature." In Jane Austen's view marriage depends on much more than mere physical comfort and material security.

Chapter 20 (I, 20)   When Mr. Collins informs Mrs. Bennet of Elizabeth's declining his proposal, she is stunned, and tries to enlist her husband's aid in getting Lizzy to change her mind. With customary good humor, Mr. Bennet tells Elizabeth, "Your mother will never see you again if you do not marry Mr. Collins, and I will never see you again if you do." Mrs. Bennet remains in a distraught mood all day, alternately accusing Elizabeth of treachery, bewailing her fate as a mother of five, and apologizing extravagantly to Mr. Collins. He unctuously reminds her that "resignation to inevitable evils is the duty of us all."

COMMENTARY: The economic motif of Elizabeth's situation rises to the surface in this chapter. While criticizing Elizabeth, Mrs. Bennet says "I am sure I do not know who is to maintain you when your father is dead. *I* shall not be able to keep you." The reader is made aware of Elizabeth's spiritual courage in having rejected the material comforts extended to her by Collins. Note also that Charlotte Lucas has been informed of the ludicrous events of the day.

Chapter 21 (I, 21)   The Bennet household settles into an uncomfortable silence after the fiasco of the proposal. Collins' departure is eagerly awaited by everyone, with the possible exception of Mrs. Bennet. At this point Jane is grieved by a note from Caroline: according to her, Bingley's stay in London has been extended (probably through the winter), and everyone now has hopes of seeing the future marriage of him and Miss Darcy. Elizabeth immediately sees that Caroline is attempting to discourage Jane and surmises that Bingley is being kept from Jane.

COMMENTARY: As well as showing us Caroline's unpleasant character, this chapter offers a further contrast between the two Bennet sisters. Whereas Jane is soft, trusting, and guileless, Elizabeth is perceptive and clever. Jane is easily disturbed by her emotions; Elizabeth is fairly stable and durable. Elizabeth sees that Caroline's letter is, at best, a display of ignorance, and most likely an attempt to discourage Jane from pursuing Bingley further. The best guess is that Caroline hopes to get Bingley married to Miss Darcy, so that the path may be cleared for her own marriage to Darcy. Jane is totally naive about such worldly maneuverings and must be shown the way by her younger sister.

The chapter is, of course, important for plot purposes in that the separation of Bingley and Jane becomes more serious; the reader's suspense is raised by the thought of this additional barrier to their union.

Chapter 22 (I, 22) Elizabeth has been grateful to Charlotte Lucas for entertaining Mr. Collins in the days after his debacle. His brief acquaintance with Charlotte is sufficient for the wife-hungry Collins: he proposes, and is accepted! Elizabeth is stunned. Not only is she aware of the absurdity of "Mr. Collins' making two offers of marriage within three days," but, more upsetting, her best friend has accepted the proposal of this ridiculous man.

COMMENTARY: The economic basis of marriage is emphasized in this chapter. Jane Austen shows clearly that the Lucas family feel triumphant about the proposal of Mr. Collins; they are ready and anxious to sacrifice their daughter to a fool in order to guarantee her economic security. The proposal is also a financial boon to the brothers and sisters, who not only have the family estate to themselves now, but also the likelihood of the family's coming into possession of Longbourn, the estate belonging to their friends!

As for Charlotte, she is prepared with the usual rationalizations. She confesses that she is not a "romantic," and desires only a "comfortable home;" she is also contented with Mr. Collins' "character, connections and situation." Jane Austen is not a "romantic" either, but she clearly disapproves of a marriage based on such flimsy materialistic grounds. Charlotte stands as a contrast to Elizabeth: both are young girls without economic security, but one sacrifices her life and security for financial comfort. The fact that Charlotte was once Elizabeth's best friend is an indication of her former true worth and an example of how even the best characters can be corrupted by such considerations.

Chapter 23 (l, 23)   Sir William Lucas arrives to inform the Bennet family of the engagement. There is some embarrassment when Lydia tactlessly reveals that Mr. Collins has just recently proposed to Elizabeth. When Mr. Lucas leaves, the fury of Mrs. Bennet is unleashed: an eligible bachelor has been trapped by the competitor. Mr. Bennet is relieved, however, to know that Charlotte Lucas is "as foolish as his wife and more foolish than his daughter." The friendship of Charlotte and Elizabeth seems to disintegrate, and the atmosphere at Longbourn is oppressive. Worst of all, Bingley has not yet written, and even Elizabeth fears that "his sisters would be successful in keeping him away."

COMMENTARY: The rivalries between families is brought out plainly in this chapter: the Lucas family has temporarily defeated the Bennet family in catching a man for their daughter. Meanwhile, Elizabeth, having seen her best friend succumb to the lures of a marriage of convenience, is unusually pessimistic about Jane's affair with Bingley. Her despondency may be a result of her own loss of a prospective suitor, for in such an atmosphere she cannot be wholly immune to the economic arguments of her mother.

COMMENTARY: Volume 1   Chapter 23 brings to a conclusion the first volume of *Pride and Prejudice* as was originally published. It will be helpful to take stock of the progress of the novel to this point.

By now, the reader has encountered all the major characters. He has a fairly clear idea of the personalities of Elizabeth, Jane, and the rest of the Bennet family. He has met the males of the story—Darcy, Bingley, Collins, and Wickham. The only character about whom there may be some confusion is Darcy; the careless reader, willing to accept the judgment of Elizabeth, is apt to misread Darcy's character. Thus the reader must move, with the heroine, to a full understanding of Darcy's strengths and a recognition of Elizabeth's faults. The reader, in other words, must come to recognize and understand the qualities of pride and prejudice.

As with any novel, the lives of the major characters do not run smoothly. The first volume ends at a very black moment; all seems destroyed or threatened. Charlotte's marriage to Mr. Collins seems to be undeniable evidence of the economic forces which control human lives. On a lower scale, human antagonists are hindering the happiness of the Bennet girls. Elizabeth has no doubt that Darcy and Caroline Bingley are deliberately obstructing the course of Bingley's true love. Furthermore there is the embarrassing intrusion of Mrs. Bennet, whose gaucheries threaten to drive off all eligible suitors within hearing distance. Finally, there are internal flaws which prevent the happiness of the main characters. First among these is Elizabeth's prejudice against Darcy, a result of her curious failure to penetrate beyond the external appearances of Wickham and Darcy. All of these antagonists have been established in the first volume and must be defeated in the remainder of the novel.

Chapter 24 (II, 1)   The gloom of chapter 23 is deepened by a letter from Caroline Bingley informing Jane that the party now plans to remain in London through the winter. A conversation with Elizabeth ensues, during which Jane insists that she will resign herself to fate: she is now sure that she had overestimated Bingley's affection for her, and she defends Miss Bingley and Darcy against Elizabeth's accusations. Elizabeth sadly acquiesces to Jane's wish that Bingley not be mentioned again. Meanwhile Wickham is something of a hero in Meryton: his story of persecution at the hands of Darcy has been accepted by everyone.

COMMENTARY: The plot takes another bad turn with the definite extension of Bingley's stay in London. This is the second example of Bingley's inconstancy, of how "little dependence can be placed on the *appearance* of either merit or sense." Nevertheless, Elizabeth still fails to see through Darcy's *appearance,* and it is left to the naive Jane to defend him.

Chapter 25 (II, 2)   Mr. and Mrs. Gardiner (Mrs. Bennet's brother and sister-in-law) visit Longbourn for Christmas. Elizabeth relates to her aunt the story of Jane's unhappy affair with Bingley, and Mrs. Gardiner suggests that a visit to London might improve Jane's spirits. Elizabeth approves of the plan but she sees no hope in the proximity of Jane to

Bingley: she is cynical about Bingley's soft character, the snobbery of Darcy, and the maliciousness of Caroline. Mrs. Gardiner
suspects from her observations that there is a growing attach-
ment between Elizabeth and Wickham, who has been seen frequently with her in public.

COMMENTARY: The plot begins to move again with the arrival of
the Gardiners. At the end of the last chapter, the
situation was stagnant, especially because of the distance
separating Bingley from Longbourn. Now, with the promise of Jane's visit to London, there is a distinct possibility
that the two may meet and be reconciled in spite of Darcy
and Caroline.

Notice the implicit attack by Jane Austen on contemporary notions of "romantic love." Mrs. Gardiner sees
that such love, based on "feelings" and "passion," is swift
and violent, but also vague, unpredictable, and brief. Jane
Austen's philosophy demands a love that is more perma-
nent and sensible.

Chapter 26 (II, 3) Elizabeth reassures Mrs. Gardiner that she is
not in love with Wickham, attractive though
he may be, and that she will certainly consider all factors before
taking any action. The Gardiners depart for London with Jane.
Charlotte, before marrying Collins, invites Elizabeth to visit
frequently at Hunsford Parsonage, but Elizabeth is now certain
that she and Charlotte can no longer enjoy "the comfort of inti-
macy." Letters from Jane soon reveal that Caroline is aware of
Jane's presence in London; just as clearly, Caroline is hiding this
information from her brother. Jane now realizes how badly mistaken she was in her estimate of Caroline's character, while
Elizabeth is all the more infuriated at Bingley for permitting
himself to be duped.

COMMENTARY: The reader sees with Elizabeth that Jane has
matured in the process of being disillusioned:
until now she has naively trusted everyone, but Bingley's
failure to see her in London is convincing evidence that
there is "a strong appearance of duplicity." Jane Austen's
favorite theme of self-education and growth is thus developed in this small sub-plot. Elizabeth, ironically, reveals

that she is still hasty in her judgments and subject to prejudice. She must show growth of character also.

Chapter 27 (II, 4)   In March, Elizabeth starts out on a trip to Hunsford, accompanied by Sir William Lucas and his daughter Maria. She discovers at the Gardiners' home that Jane suffers from periodic bouts of dejection. She relates to Mrs. Gardiner that Wickham is now courting a certain Miss King, who has come into a fortune of 10,000 pounds. Mrs. Gardiner disapproves of Wickham's "mercenary motives" for marrying, and Elizabeth defends him good-naturedly. They both make plans for a future trip to the Lake country.

COMMENTARY: The economic motives for marrying are again stressed, this time from the male point of view: Wickham, cut off from his fortune, must abandon Elizabeth—if he was ever serious about her—and turn to more fruitful grounds. Elizabeth is so familiar with the system that she seems quite resigned to being abandoned by Wickham. (In the last paragraph, Jane Austen satirizes the growing mode of "romantic" or "imaginative" literature.)

Notice also the thoroughness with which Jane Austen has developed Elizabeth's state of mind at the time when she is to depart for Hunsford. The heroine has reached an important point in her development; the visit to Hunsford will be a resting point where she can compose herself after a number of unhappy experiences. Elizabeth now is in an abandoned, exposed position, without any real emotional support behind her, and heading in the direction of "enemy" territory. Her family continues to be unsympathetic: her mother and father have probably never been congenial, and even Jane is now engrossed in her own affairs. Jane's particularly gloomy mood at this point—a result of Bingley's departure—is shared by her sister.

Elizabeth has also lost the support of her friend Charlotte, whose marriage to Collins has betrayed all the values which she and Elizabeth once agreed on. The heroine is also disturbed by the recent loss of two potential mates: Wickham's interest has shifted to Miss King, and even Mr. Collins was a man, for all that. Elizabeth is probably afraid that Mr. Collins has turned into a decent enough husband and that Hunsford Parsonage might be more pleasant than she had predicted. Finally, she is unhappy about her relationship with Darcy and nervous because she has discovered that she will meet his aunt, Lady Catherine.

All of these elements are present in Elizabeth's character at this juncture. The reader can only marvel that Jane Austen has recognized them, organized them, and woven them together into a coherent portrait of the heroine at the moment when she is being uprooted. It is one example of the novelist's penetrating insight and subtle artistry.

Chapter 28 (II, 5)   Elizabeth travels to Hunsford Parsonage, which is attached to Rosings Park, Lady Catherine de Bourgh's estate. Elizabeth is welcomed by Charlotte and Collins, who has not changed at all. Elizabeth discovers that life at Hunsford is awkward and uncomfortably embarrassing for Charlotte, but that she manages to suffer the fool, her husband, silently. Shortly after her arrival, Elizabeth meets Miss de Bourgh, a "thin and small" creature who looks "sickly and cross," and therefore, Elizabeth thinks, would make a proper wife for Darcy.

COMMENTARY: Here is Jane Austen's portrayal of the results of a marriage founded on convenience: Charlotte's home is indeed "neat and comfortable," but she must also "wisely" be deaf to the foolishness of her husband. One sips bitter soup in a household where no true affection exists. Only when Mr. Collins "is forgotten, was there really a great air of comfort throughout." This is Jane Austen's most bitter indictment of the marriage customs of England, where a girl must sell herself in order to find room and board.

Chapter 29 (II, 6)   The people at Hunsford Parsonage are invited to Rosings Park for dinner. In spite of Collins' ominous warnings about Lady Catherine's great rank and high standards of decency, Elizabeth is equal to the confrontation. The evening is nearly a total disaster: Lady Catherine monopolizes the conversation, is dictatorial toward everyone, and impertinent with her questions. Elizabeth salvages part of her self-respect by refusing to answer an unmannerly question about her age.

COMMENTARY: This chapter is devoted to the appearance of Lady Catherine de Bourgh, one of the truly obnoxious characters in English fiction. She is an appropriate supervisor for Mr. Collins—large, offensive, loud, foolish, and tyrannical. Until now she has apparently subdued everyone she has met, and we applaud heartily Elizabeth's method of confounding the grande dame. (Elizabeth's contempt for the lushness of Rosings Park may be an indication of the growth of her personality.)

Chapter 30 (II, 7)   After the departure of the Lucases, Elizabeth stays on at Hunsford and fits herself into the dull routine of the household. Shortly before Easter, Darcy arrives with a few male relatives for a visit to Rosings.

COMMENTARY: This is an important plot event since it brings Elizabeth in contact with Darcy again; we may hope that some sort of peace between them can be arranged. This is, incidentally, one of the few times that we see Jane Austen resort to coincidence in the novel; the coincidence of Darcy's arrival at the very time that Elizabeth is visiting is not outrageous, however.

Chapter 31 (II, 8)   Elizabeth and the Collinses are invited to Rosings Park for an evening. There she quickly wins the admiration of Darcy's cousin, Fitzwilliam, with a display of wit, intelligence, and affability. Darcy and Elizabeth engage in some good-natured repartee.

COMMENTARY: Notice the careful contrast to the earlier chapters: now it is Elizabeth who shines in a strange house while Darcy observes, and now it is Darcy's relative, Lady Catherine, who embarrasses everyone with her chatter. Colonel Fitzwilliam's interest in Elizabeth again reveals to Darcy how admirable this girl really is, and how numerous her virtues. One detects in this chapter a slight movement toward each other, as when Darcy and she agree that "neither of us perform to strangers." They are indeed well-mated, but their love must have more growth.

Paradoxically, they renew their fencing with each other at the same time that they discover their admiration: confident of herself, Elizabeth skewers Darcy very neatly during the brilliant conversation.

Chapter 32 (II, 9)   Darcy accidentally finds Elizabeth alone one day, and they discuss at some length Bingley's stay in London. On succeeding days, the people at Rosings mingle with those at the parsonage, much to the perturbation of Charlotte and Elizabeth, who are puzzled by Darcy's frequent visits. Charlotte suspects that Darcy is in love with Elizabeth, a notion which Elizabeth finds ridiculous.

COMMENTARY: Elizabeth continues to be blind to the best qualities of Darcy; he, in turn, is obviously falling in love with her. The main clue to his true feelings is his sudden outburst, "You cannot have been always at Longbourn." That is, in his view, she impresses him as possessing an incredibly fine nature, for all the limitations of her rural upbringing.

Chapter 33 (II, 10)   On a walk near Rosings, Elizabeth meets Colonel Fitzwilliam. Their chat is so amiable that for a moment Elizabeth thinks that he is falling in love with her. When the conversation turns to Darcy, Elizabeth is shocked to hear of his recent boast that he had "saved a friend from the inconveniences of a most imprudent marriage." Elizabeth criticizes Darcy's officious personality, then returns to her room where she seethes over the injustice done to her sister.

COMMENTARY: By a coincidence which we are willing to accept, Elizabeth comes into another important piece of information: Darcy's admission of interfering in Bingley's affairs serves to further alienate him from Elizabeth. Given Elizabeth's character—protective of Jane, quick to misjudge people, and already prejudiced against Darcy— we are prepared for her furious reaction. She is now certain that the main cause of Jane's misfortune is Darcy; it is particularly his proud contempt for a girl from the lower classes—a girl with "one uncle who was a country attorney and another who was in business"—that Elizabeth resents.

Chapter 34 (II, 11)   Elizabeth is alone reading a gloomy letter from Jane when Darcy suddenly enters, hastens through the usual amenities, and then declares his love for her! To the reader this is no great surprise; to Elizabeth it is staggering. She recovers sufficiently to refuse his proposal in a brusque, insulting manner, and accuses him of two crimes which she can never forgive: he has destroyed Jane's hopes of marriage to Bingley, and he has mistreated Wickham villainously. Darcy makes no attempt to answer her accusations and quickly retreats, leaving Elizabeth to a few confused impressions of what has occurred.

COMMENTARY: This chapter is about halfway through the novel, and with it comes to an end the steady growth of the separation between Elizabeth and Darcy. Ever since the first chapter, with only a few halts along the way, the two have grown further and further apart; from here on in, the situation can only improve, and their lines of movement must converge. Note that this seemingly catastrophic argument occurs at an ironic moment: Darcy simultaneously reveals his love for Elizabeth just as she discovers how much she hates him.

Undoubtedly, it is Darcy who is more nearly blameless here. True, his proposal is rather pompous and self-centered: it certainly is not one which appeals to Elizabeth, and it even bears uncomfortable similarities to Mr. Collins' proposal. But now, Darcy is willing to ignore Elizabeth's economic status (not an inconsiderable factor in arranging marriages, as we have seen); in spite of her family background and her class, Elizabeth now appears to be an ideal woman to marry. Elizabeth is as obtuse as ever. She sees no inconsistency in accusing Darcy of snobbery toward her sister when he has just proposed to her. All she can say of the situation is "his pride, his abominable pride." She has much to learn.

Chapter 35 (II, 12)   Elizabeth meets Darcy on a walk and he hands her a letter. In it he explains his part in the two situations which have offended her. On the subject of Jane and Bingley, he seems unrepentant, claiming that in his opinion such a match did not appear beneficial for Bingley. He defends himself only briefly, explaining that Jane had always appeared "indifferent" to Bingley's attentions. (This is the same point which Charlotte had warned Elizabeth about. I, 6.) He defends himself more fully on the subject of Wickham, saying that the scoundrel had squandered the 3,000 pounds Darcy had given him, and had attempted to gain a larger fortune by wooing Darcy's sister.

COMMENTARY: This letter is the turning point in the novel; unless the novel comes to an immediate close, the letter will probably draw Darcy and Elizabeth together. It is significant that Darcy, the male, is more enlightened, open-minded, and sensible than Elizabeth; after the humiliating interview, he would have been justified in being as unbending as she. That he does write the letter is a sign of his wisdom and generous spirit. Where Darcy thinks himself right, he states so bluntly, without any attempt to apologize or excuse himself. He is also willing to admit where he may have been wrong. The letter, at the least, shows how complex the truth is, and reveals that Elizabeth has seen the situation only from one limited vantage point. Elizabeth must feel the justice of Darcy's calm analysis, "Ignorant as you previously were of everything . . ." From that moment on, Elizabeth begins to grow toward wisdom.

Chapter 36 (II, 13) Elizabeth ponders the contents of the letter again and again. Although she discounts Darcy's explanations at first, she gradually sees that she may have erred in judgment, first of Wickham's character, then of Darcy's treatment of Jane. As she comes to recognize her own blindness, Darcy, ironically, is departing from Rosings Park.

COMMENTARY: This is a chapter that illustrates the 18th century virtues of cold logic and reason. There is no sentiment, wild passion, or impulsive surrender either by Darcy or Elizabeth. The chapter is structured beautifully, showing the movement of Elizabeth's mind from the simpler problems (those affecting her less directly) to the more complex, more personal problems. First she analyzes Darcy's relations with Wickham; the two stories being irreconcilable, Elizabeth is at an impasse until she realizes that Wickham has acted indecorously by revealing his story to her on the night they met. She now surmises that Wickham had told a lie in order to deceive the community for his own purposes. His courtship of Miss King, the heiress, seems indisputable proof of his guilt.

Darcy's character undergoes a steady improvement in her opinion. No one who knew Darcy (except Wickham) had ever spoken ill of him; on the contrary, she sees that Wickhams' story appealed to her exactly because he had flattered her whereas Darcy had not, when they had first met. The truth is blinding: she has "courted prepossession and ignorance and driven reason away where either were concerned." This is the important "recognition" of the novel: she now sees how "despicably" she has acted.

She also analyzes Darcy's intervention in Bingley's affair, and sees that there is justice in his actions: Jane indeed had given no outward display of her affection, and the Bennet family had done its unconscious best to drive all eligible suitors away from Longbourn.

Through a process of self-education and experience, Jane Austen's heroine has begun to mature, to cast off her prejudices. Whether she can be reconciled to Darcy is still open to question.

Chapter 37 (II, 14)   Elizabeth determines to leave for home after her six-week stay at Hunsford. Her thoughts run continually over Darcy's letter; although she can recognize the reasonableness of his view, she cannot forgive him his earlier insults. She is most discouraged about her own family, which she realizes has contributed to Jane's unhappiness.

COMMENTARY: Elizabeth is now willing to admit that Jane's blighted romance is largely due to the Bennet family, and not to Darcy. Her brief absence from home has provided Elizabeth with a certain detachment in relation to her family. Her father now appears to have been totally irresponsible, her mother incredibly gauche, and her sisters incorrigibly naive. The chapter reveals Elizabeth growing painfully in another direction: she possesses that knowledge that pains all of us—the knowledge that our immediate family is not perfect.

Chapter 38 (II, 15)   Elizabeth and Maria Lucas leave Hunsford Parsonage for the trip home. Elizabeth is sad to leave Charlotte, the dear friend who seems trapped in an impossible situation; Elizabeth consoles herself with the thought that Charlotte had married "with her eyes open" and seems contented enough. Within four hours Elizabeth and Maria are at the Gardiner house in London, where they are to spend the next few days.

COMMENTARY: In spite of its subject matter — travelling — this chapter is a resting point after the exertions of the past four chapters. The past is all important, as Elizabeth admits, when she thinks of "how much I shall have to conceal."

Chapter 39 (II, 16)   On the trip home, Elizabeth and Jane are met by their two youngest sisters, who are bursting with the news that Miss King has left Wickham. Their arrival home is met uneffusively by Mr. Bennet: "I am glad you are come back, Lizzy."

COMMENTARY: The news that Wickham is now free is important. There is something ominous in Elizabeth's realization during the conversation that "there was no escaping the frequent mention of Wickham's name." Considering Lydia's silliness, Elizabeth has more reason for not wanting to see Wickham than she suspects.

Chapter 40 (II, 17)   Elizabeth reveals two pieces of news to Jane: that concerning Darcy's proposal, and that relating to Wickham's villainy. She does not speak of Bingley's affection for Jane, fearful that such belated news will make Jane more disconsolate than ever.

COMMENTARY: One should not miss the ironic comparison made here between Wickham and Darcy: "One has got all the goodness and the other all the appearance of it." This epitomizes Elizabeth's fault exactly, since she—among others at Meryton and Longbourn—had been taken in by Wickham's appearance and had failed to see Darcy's goodness. Elizabeth now confesses to Jane that she has made herself ridiculous as a "consequence of the prejudices I had been encouraging." Now she must keep two secrets:

she cannot tell Jane of Bingley's affection, and she cannot reveal the truth about Darcy ("it would be the death of half the good people in Meryton to attempt to place him in amiable light"). She must now pay the consequences for having been mistaken for so long. Note also that her new wisdom is not perfect: she is mistaken ˙about Wickham's impending departure, or the conditions under which that departure will occur.

Chapter 41 (II, 18)   Lydia and Kitty are downcast over the impending relocation of the regiment in Brighton. They (significantly reinforced by their mother) argue that the Bennet family should go to Brighton for a vacation. Lydia receives a sudden invitation from a Mrs. Forster (an officer's wife) to accompany her to Brighton. Elizabeth attempts to prevent Lydia's trip, seeing the need for restraining the flighty young girl. She pleads with her father to exert some discipline on Lydia or be prepared to admit that she "will soon be beyond the reach of amendment." Characteristically, Mr. Bennet argues that the experience will be of advantage to Lydia in that it will help tame her. In this vacuum of power, Lydia must have her own way.

COMMENTARY: This is an important chapter for the development of the plot since it frees Lydia from her parents' control. She is now at liberty to direct her own life, and influence the lives of others. The repercussions which grow out of this chapter will occupy most of Volume III.

Elizabeth says goodbye to Wickham, the attractive young man who was thought to be her suitor not long before. During the farewell dinner at Longbourn she drops several hints about Darcy and especially about her revaluation of Darcy's character. Wickham is now nervous about how much Elizabeth knows or about her real feelings toward him. They part, with "mutual civility and possibly a mutual desire of never meeting again."

COMMENTARY: The chapter is significantly full of Lydia and Wickham, showing what an influence they will be on the remainder of the novel. Just as important, this chapter helps the reader to measure the growth of Elizabeth Bennet. She seems to be admirably clear-sighted and responsible in her dealings with those around her. Not only does this apply to Wickham—whom she directs nicely in their last conversation—but also to her father, whose true character she is willing to admit, perhaps for the first time in her life. The aftereffects of Darcy's letter are making themselves manifest.

Chapter 42 (II, 19)   While waiting to make a trip to the Lake country, Elizabeth is morose about her father's irresponsibility, the incompatibility of her parents, and the damage their untidy marriage has done to the five Bennet girls. She anxiously awaits the arrival of the Gardiners, who are to be her travelling companions. Finally, in July they depart, heading northward; soon they find themselves in the neighborhood of Pemberley, the Darcy estate. Elizabeth has misgivings about visiting the home of the man she dislikes, but when she hears from the chambermaid at the inn that the Darcy family is not "down for the summer," she agrees to visit the estate.

COMMENTARY: Jane Austen's analysis of the Bennet family is very important, and an appropriate note on which to end Volume II. Most noticeable here is Jane Austen's implied criticism of Mr. Bennet. For some critics, he is an entirely attractive and sympathetic figure; he is not so for Jane Austen or Elizabeth. He has made an unwise choice of a wife—who must have been as pretty and as stupid as Lydia in her youth—and now feels no affection for her. (Note the comparison between Charlotte Lucas and Mr. Bennet: if a woman may purchase security at the cost of domestic unhappiness, a man may pay the same price for a pretty face.) Worse, he has even abandoned his responsibilities as a parent; comfortable and detached, he occupies a lofty position and watches the absurdities occurring in the Bennet household. Such detachment has succeeded only in ruining his children, four of them probably permanently. Mary, Lydia, and Kitty are lacking in some quality, and there is real doubt whether Jane will be able to handle the challenges of the world. Only one—Elizabeth herself—has a potential for development that has not been completely stifled by her parents. In fact, even she has been a failure so far in her dealings with other people.

The trip in the direction of Pemberley is obviously contrived by the novelist to help the heroine correct the errors she has made so far.

COMMENTARY: *Volume II*   As Volume II comes to an end, the
reader is aware of a promise and a
threat. The threat is implicit in the worsening situation at
Longbourn: Lydia's departure from the protective custody
of her father automatically creates a dangerous situation.
The alert reader will be aware of the catastrophe which
threatens to develop out of Lydia's vacation at Brighton.

The promise which we sense at the end of Volume
II is only a matter of degree. In many ways, the situation
is as unpromising as that at the end of Volume I. Jane and
Bingley are still separated, and their situation is even more
aggravated by the passage of time. Elizabeth and Darcy
are still separated, and their relationship is even more
exacerbated by his inept proposal and her haughty rejection.

Yet, there has been growth and movement toward
wisdom throughout Volume II. Elizabeth has shown herself capable of handling the hostility of society at large—
as represented by Lady Catherine. She at least recognizes
the unworthiness of Wickham, whereas not long before
she had toyed with the idea of accepting him as a suitor.
She is even cognizant of Darcy's good qualities, a painful
admission for Elizabeth to make. One might say that Elizabeth has become a more attractive heroine for having
passed through the baptism of fire; the reader may now
anticipate that the laws of poetic justice will operate to
bring Elizabeth and Fitzwilliam Darcy together.

Although Volume II ends on a seemingly melancholy note, the movement toward Pemberley is symbolic
of the gradual rapprochement of the hero and heroine.

Chapter 43 (III, 1)   The Gardiners and Elizabeth visit Pemberley; inside the house, they are guided by the
housekeeper, Mrs. Reynolds, who praises Darcy so effusively that
Elizabeth wonders if this is the same man. After they leave the
house, Elizabeth is shocked to meet Darcy on the grounds of the
estate. He has returned home unexpectedly. She is vexed and
embarrassed by the coincidental meeting, all the more because
Darcy seems so hospitable and decent. When they are alone,
finally, Darcy asks Elizabeth if he might introduce her to his

sister. Georgiana Darcy will be arriving at Pemberley the following day in the company of Mr. Bingley and his sisters.

COMMENTARY: Elizabeth's shock at the apparent change in Darcy is easily explained: the change is internal, not external, and it is not Darcy who has changed but Elizabeth. The scales have fallen from her eyes, and she now sees him as he really is. Her trust in appearances—which has misled her for so long about Wickham and Darcy—has proven faulty; through experience, the testimony of others, and her good sense, she has arrived at a truer estimate of Darcy's character. That Elizabeth's discovery (and self-discovery) has not come too late is hinted by Darcy's wish to introduce her to his sister: the presentation of an intended spouse to the family was an inevitable part of the elaborate social code. For the first time in the novel, then, there is real hope for reconciliation; as Volume III opens, the paths of Darcy and Elizabeth begin to converge.

Chapter 44 (III, 2)   With trepidation, Elizabeth meets Georgiana Darcy. Shortly thereafter she greets Bingley and quickly modifies her harsh views of him when he shows an interest in the welfare of Jane. More testimony is heard from the neighbors about Darcy's good reputation and Wickham's notorious treachery. Elizabeth continues to reexamine her original prejudice against Darcy and quickly comes to feel respect and gratitude toward him. She realizes now that he probably loves her and wonders if she can ever love him.

COMMENTARY: The long period of darkness seems over. Elizabeth is well on her way to accepting Darcy's good character unquestioningly. The Cinderella theme is almost complete: a not very attractive young girl of unpromising family and background is about to be rescued by the prince. Significantly, as this liaison is about to be consolidated, the affair of Jane and Bingley takes a turn for the better, showing how much other affairs are dependent on the relationship between the two leading characters.

Chapter 45 (III, 3)   Elizabeth meets Caroline Bingley, who is with her brother at Pemberley. Caroline has not changed at all; during the conversation she makes several

sardonic remarks about the regiment at Meryton. Alone with
Darcy, she again attempts to undermine his obvious affection for
Elizabeth.

COMMENTARY: Note that Caroline accuses Darcy of once having
had an unfavorable opinion of Elizabeth Bennet,
when he had known her only briefly. Caroline seems to
imply that Darcy would have done better to retain this
earlier view. Darcy admits to the justice of Caroline's
accusation, although he denies her conclusion: his bad
opinion "was only when I first knew her, for it is many
months since I have considered her as one of the handsom-
est women in my acquaintance." This statement epitomizes
the main theme of the book: Darcy and Elizabeth have
discovered their love only after establishing it firmly on a
foundation of experience and mutual understanding.
"Love at first sight" is a pleasant notion for foolish minds,
but it cannot be a dependable guide for marriage.

Chapter 46 (III, 4)   Elizabeth's conquest of Darcy is suddenly
interrupted by the arrival of shocking news
from Jane: Lydia has eloped with Wickham. Worse, in a second
letter that follows immediately, there is doubt whether the young
couple are indeed married. Why should Wickham, whose motives
have always been so uncompromisingly materialistic, run off with
the youngest girl in a family without any real wealth? It appears
from Jane's letter that Longbourn is in utter chaos: even Mr.
Bennet has risen from his easy chair and gone to London to find
his daughter.

COMMENTARY: The elopement will have several ramifications
later in the novel, but it is interesting to note that
the first use to which Jane Austen puts the event is as a
criticism of Mr. Bennet. The consequences of his "neglect
and mistaken indulgence" are coming to haunt him now;
even Jane is able to say that she "never in my life saw him
so affected." At best, Lydia has embarrassed the family by
her eccentric behavior. At worst, she has created a major
scandal for the Bennets by running off to live with a lover
without benefit of marriage.

Elizabeth relates the news to Darcy and informs him that
she must leave for Longbourn immediately He is thoughtful,

sober, shocked by the turn of events. Elizabeth realizes that whatever chances she had of winning him are now lost. Lydia's foolishness and the impending scandal have brought ruin to her whole family, especially to Jane and Elizabeth.

COMMENTARY: This section illustrates perfectly the 18th century emphasis on the mutual responsibilities of members of any family. In the 20th century, an individual is primarily responsible for himself, and there is no axiom asserting that the guilt of a person is shared by members of his family. In Jane Austen's age family pride, family honor, and family responsibilities are powerful factors in morality. And so Elizabeth immediately thinks that the impropriety committed by Lydia has somehow tainted the lives of the other Bennet sisters. She finds her worst suspicions confirmed in the dark silence of Darcy shortly after he hears the news.

However, the reader must note the ambiguity of Darcy's silence. Darcy at this moment may be feeling exactly what Elizabeth is feeling at that moment: a sense of guilt for not having met an obligation to a young person, for Wickham had been not unlike a younger brother to Darcy several years before. Elizabeth's fears of losing Darcy may thus be groundless.

Chapter 47 (III, 5) On the trip to Longbourn, Mr. Gardiner seems optimistic: he cannot believe Wickham so vicious as not to marry Lydia. Elizabeth is pessimistic: Wickham has already shown himself totally dedicated to only one thing, the pursuit of wealth. Nor does that young man have anything to fear from an irate father: Mr. Bennet's indolence will prevent him from taking any positive action, as it has many times in the past. As for Lydia, Elizabeth concludes that Lydia will forever be immature and empty-headed.

COMMENTARY: This section shows Elizabeth indulging in a merciless analysis of her family; her clear vision, good sense, and judgment are at work exposing all their faults. She now confesses readily that until recently she had been "ignorant of the truth" about Wickham, had even considered herself in love with him. She finds herself most culpable in that she concealed all she knew about him after her return from Hunsford Parsonage (and Darcy's letter); most regrettably, she had failed to warn Lydia before her trip to Brighton. Elizabeth's analysis of the situation and her recognition of her part in the overall guilt are sure indications of her growing wisdom and maturity.

They arrive at Longbourn, where there is nothing new to be said. The young couple have lost themselves in the heart of London, and Mr. Bennet's search has been unrewarding so far. Mrs. Bennet, as expected, is busy pitying herself, accusing the others, and making excuses for Lydia, who "is not the kind of girl to do such a thing." Mr. Gardiner decides to go to London to help Mr. Bennet in the search. Elizabeth attempts to get more solid information from Jane, but instead is given an unusually silly letter from Lydia on the day of her elopement.

COMMENTARY: This section of the chapter is largely devoted to "style." Mrs. Bennet's speech reveals her as the silly old woman we have always known. Mary's platitudes are as dry, useless, and divorced from the realities of life as she is. And Lydia's letter—the diction, sentence structure, the tone—exposes her immediately as an irresponsible, foolish young girl. Once again, Jane Austen shows her interest in style as an indicator of human character.

Chapter 48 (III, 6)   The pursuit in London is still unsuccessful (perhaps symbolizing the ineptitude of Mr. Bennet), and Longbourn is in a thick gloom. At this dark moment, a condescending letter arrives from Mr. Collins, informing the Bennets that he and Lady Catherine are aware of the scandal and have concluded that the event "must be injurious to the fortunes of all the daughters." Mr. Bennet returns home, as philosophical as ever, but now recognizing the extent of his failure as a father.

COMMENTARY: Mr. Bennet's recognition is of primary importance here: he now realizes that he has been to blame, as Elizabeth had informed him "last May." The novel is thus partly the story of Mr. Bennet's awakening to his duties as a father, and parallels the growth in knowledge of Darcy and Elizabeth. His admission that

Elizabeth has shown "some greatness of mind" is a tribute which must impress any reader.

Chapter 49 (III, 7)   Mr. Gardiner informs the Bennets that he has found Lydia and Wickham. They are not yet married, but Wickham has agreed to marry Lydia upon the payment of a kind of dowry. The terms are surprisingly light: 100 pounds per annum while Mr. Bennet is alive, and Lydia's fair share of her father's 5,000 pound legacy upon his death. Elizabeth and her father are puzzled by Wickham's generosity (they know that he could have demanded more); they both agree that he is a fool "if he takes her with a farthing less than ten thousand pounds." They conclude that Mr. Gardiner has done the humane thing and supplied the difference without saying anything.

COMMENTARY: Now we see more clearly the network of inter-relationships in the family. Wickham's actions have been predicated on the knowledge that Mr. Bennet will pay blackmail in order to avoid any scandal in the family. Mr. Bennet is only too willing to *buy* the wedding, realizing that he has four other daughters to consider. Their happiness depends on their impeccable credentials as marriageable ladies, a status which is jeopardized by Lydia's foolish elopement. Even Mr. Gardiner, an uncle with children of his own, conscientiously and energetically plays a part in arranging the settlement, no doubt fearing that the stigma will spread to his branch of the family. Jane Austen is impressing on the reader the dangers, even the immorality, of egocentric actions which disregard the mutual interdependence of human society.

Chapter 50 (III, 8)   Mr. Bennet's financial situation is described in some detail, revealing that the elder Bennets have both been extravagant. Mr. Bennet sinks into his "former indolence" once the articles of marriage are arranged, but he vows never to admit the newlyweds into his house. Elizabeth meanwhile has been fully aware of her love for Darcy and is crushed by her loss.

COMMENTARY: Jane Austen gives away the main purpose of her novel in the statement that "No such happy marriage could now teach the admiring multitude what connubial felicity really was." That is, the marriage of Darcy and Elizabeth, if and when it takes place, will be an example of true wedded bliss, since from her, his "manners would be improved," and from him Elizabeth would have derived "judgment, information, and knowledge of the world."

News arrives that Wickham now plans to enter a regiment stationed in the north of England. He now has means of paying all his creditors in Meryton. Mr. Bennet relents, and the young couple are invited to Longbourn.

COMMENTARY: Note that Mr. Gardiner is unintentionally vague on the extent of his financial help while making arrangements for the marriage. Neither the reader nor Elizabeth can be certain of the details behind that arrangement.

Chapter 51 (III, 9)   Shortly after their wedding day, Wickham and Lydia arrive at Longbourn. Neither seems to be dismayed in the least by what has occurred; in fact, they seem as shallow and confident as ever. Elizabeth, Jane, and Mr. Bennet are stupefied by the idiocy of the conversation and the senseless pride of Mrs. Bennet in having a married daughter. In a conversation with Lydia a few days later, Elizabeth is surprised to hear that Darcy was at the wedding. Puzzled by the information, she writes to Mrs. Gardiner for an explanation.

COMMENTARY: Lydia redeems herself with this accidental slip of the tongue: as a result of this clue, Elizabeth will be reconciled to Darcy, since she must attempt now to discover why Darcy was at the wedding of two people whom he must have detested. Elizabeth's natural curiosity and her desire for truth will lead her to answer the question as best she can.

Chapter 52 (III, 10)   Mrs. Gardiner reveals the whole story to Elizabeth in a letter: Darcy had gone to London, traced Wickham and Lydia, and had paid the bribe to get Wickham to marry Lydia. He and Mr. Gardiner had agreed to keep the details secret, since Darcy sincerely felt guilty about being secretive long ago on the subject of Wickham's true character. Elizabeth is shocked, pleased, overwhelmed, humbled.

"Her heart did whisper that he had done it for her," but she cannot yet admit that he loves her.

COMMENTARY: Notice the strange reason for Elizabeth's reticence in admitting Darcy's love for her: Darcy would never marry her because he would then be a brother-in-law to Wickham. Once again the theme of family honor and family pride asserts itself. The chapter is very important for its clarification of the plot: we actually have an exposition of details in the past to make us understand the marriage arrangements. It seems that Elizabeth's fears of Darcy's contempt are indeed groundless, and that only a few barriers remain between them.

Chapter 53 (III, 11) Lydia and Wickham depart, presumably not to return for two or three years. Several days later, the Bennets hear a rumor that Mr. Bingley is returning to Netherfield to do some hunting. Shortly afterward, both Darcy and Bingley arrive at Longbourn to pay their respects. Elizabeth knows now that Darcy approves of Bingley's match with Jane, and she is close to admitting that Darcy is still interested in her. However, their first meeting is awkward—as usual—because Darcy is shy and uncommunicative; both are embarrassed by Mrs. Bennet's steady stream of nonsense. Elizabeth consoles herself with the knowledge that Bingley has recovered his interest in Jane.

COMMENTARY: Although not much happens, this chapter is important for the plot. As Elizabeth recognizes, Darcy's arrival at Longbourn is a signal that his affection for her has not been destroyed by the Lydia-Wickham escapade. His motives are not examined and his state of mind remains concealed, but the reader assumes from his actions that his love for Elizabeth is intact. The two men at Netherfield are now in a favorable position to be caught by the ladies at Longbourn.

Chapter 54 (III, 12) Elizabeth is puzzled by Darcy's brooding silence. His coolness toward her continues at a dinner party given at Longbourn the next Tuesday. Bingley and Jane renew their acquaintance (giving Elizabeth a "triumphant sensation"), but Darcy remains unsociable, even indifferent.

COMMENTARY: Jane Austen begins to relax the suspense some-
                    what by bringing Jane and Bingley together, but
the union of Elizabeth and Darcy must take a little longer.
Once again, appearances deceive Elizabeth, making her
fear the worst, when she should be more understanding
about his shyness. A measure of Elizabeth's growth since
the beginning of the novel is that she now recognizes
Darcy's fundamental decency.

Chapter 55 (III, 13)   Darcy leaves for London, and Bingley re-
                             mains alone at Netherfield. Within a short
time, Bingley renews his old acquaintances in the area. In no
time at all, he proposes to Jane. The earlier misfortunes of the
Bennet family are quite forgotten. Mr. Bennet approves whole-
heartedly of his prospective son-in-law; Mrs. Bennet is ecstatic
over the capture of such an eligible bachelor; and Elizabeth is
happy in Jane's good fortune. Elizabeth jokes about her own
spinsterhood, saying that her only hope is to capture another Mr.
Collins.

COMMENTARY: Mr. Bennet reflects Jane Austen's opinion when
                    he says that the marriage of Jane and Bingley
will probably be successful because of their similar personalities. However, being too "complying," "easy," and
"generous," they lack the wisdom of Darcy and Elizabeth.
They are too easily manipulated by other people, and will
probably need the companionship and protection of Darcy
and Elizabeth for some time. The chapter is important, in
any case, in that one important line of the sub-plot is concluded.

Chapter 56 (III, 14)   Lady Catherine de Bourgh arrives at Long-
                             bourn, enraged and prepared for a battle
with Elizabeth. She has heard a rumor that Elizabeth and Darcy
are engaged. The ogress threatens, demands, cajoles, pleads in an
attempt to get Elizabeth to liquidate the engagement, which, of
course, Elizabeth knows nothing about. Elizabeth is more than
a match for Lady Catherine, who leaves in an apoplectic state,
voicing threats against Elizabeth and the whole Bennet family.

COMMENTARY: Lady Catherine's arguments are based on con-
                    siderations of family and social status. The en-
gagement of her daughter to Darcy was a forgone conclu-

sion many years before. Such planning is done for the sake of the family, not for the impulsive desires of any individual. Elizabeth's main crime, in Lady Catherine's view, is social-climbing, attempting to rise above her class; she and the Bennet family are guilty of "upstart pretensions" since they choose not to remain in the social class where they have been placed. Lady Catherine represents the traditional views of the rigid class structure of an earlier age, a structure with inflexible boundaries between the classes. She fails to realize that the love between Darcy and Elizabeth is *not* a result of impulsive desire, nor a reflection of Elizabeth's social ambitions, but rather the union of two sensible people who are eminently compatible.

Chapter 57 (III, 15) Elizabeth is now disturbed by the rumor: she knows nothing of any engagement. She also fears that if Lady Catherine appeals to Darcy with the argument of family honor, he will very likely recognize the good sense behind it; he is, after all, a person who has "notions of dignity." Meanwhile Mr. Bennet is amused by the rumor; he has received a letter from Collins which ridicules the idea of Darcy's being engaged to a peasant girl like Elizabeth.

COMMENTARY: This chapter shows Elizabeth suspended in a state of confusion; she herself, lacking any information, does not know what to think about her present relationship with Darcy. At this point she still does not know Darcy fully: she reminds herself that he has "notions of dignity," and will consider his own dignity, and family position, before marrying a girl from a lower class. She herself can recognize the validity of such arguments (she has been scarred by Lydia's selfishness), yet she is hurt by the fact that even her father can ridicule the idea of Darcy's ever loving her.

Chapter 58 (III, 16) Darcy returns to Longbourn. On a walk together, Elizabeth and Darcy discuss openly all that has happened. Elizabeth begins by thanking Darcy for his services in the Lydia-Wickham scandal. Shortly they are both admitting to their own faults and absolving each other of all blame in their bumpy relations. Darcy dredges up the events of the past, and thanks Elizabeth for having taught him a "lesson" and having properly "humbled" him.

COMMENTARY: The plot reaches its conclusion in this chapter;
                although nothing is said about a marriage, all the
indications are present (it is implicit in the discussion of
Lady Catherine's defeat), and in the next chapter we hear
that there is an engagement. The mention of the letter at
Hunsford—the explanation of its content, the motive behind it, its effect—is proof of its central importance in this
novel. After a long separation, two people have found
each other after a process of trial and error, experience,
and increasing self-knowledge. (The cynical reader may
ask if such difficulties are prerequisites for all happy marriages! The only answer possible is that Jane Austen is
primarily a novelist who is interested in specific cases
rather than in the prescription of universal remedies!)

Chapter 59 (III, 17)   Elizabeth tells Jane that she is engaged, a
                        revelation that stuns Jane, who has always
thought that Elizabeth detested Darcy. That evening, Darcy
informs Mr. Bennet, who for a moment thinks that his daughter
has lost her mind. She must explain to her father, mother, and
sisters that they have all been in error about Darcy's true character and that they are all obligated to him for his help in re-
solving the crisis brought on by Lydia. Mrs. Bennet is overwhelmed by the sudden good fortune of her second daughter,
and is perfectly ready to revise her opinion of Mr. Darcy.

COMMENTARY: In this chapter the theme of appearance and
                reality is developed from a different angle: Eliza-
beth now has the task of teaching others how to "see"
Darcy, a job made difficult because until now she herself
had "appeared" to hate him. Jane Austen's conclusion is
that as a result of the misunderstandings, her two main
characters will have a successful marriage: their "affection
was not the work of a day but had stood the test of many
months' suspense."

Chapter 60 (III, 18)   Elizabeth and Darcy talk to each other
                        about how and when their love began and
grew. They write letters to Mrs. Gardiner and Lady Catherine to
relate the good news. Mr. Bennet takes malicious delight in
writing to Collins about Darcy's good luck. Shortly thereafter
the Collinses arrive from Hunsford, fleeing the wrath of Lady
Catherine. The two couples are surrounded by well-wishers.

COMMENTARY: Notice that in Jane Austen's world there is very little passion. Someone had said that there are six kisses in her novels, none of them between lovers. Darcy and Elizabeth seem contented to talk, analyze, reason over their love; their emotions are under tight control. The modern reader is likely to find the atmosphere a bit chilly for his taste.

Chapter 61 (III, 19)   The marriages take place; the two couples settle down in the unusually blissful state of matrimony. As time passes, Elizabeth and Jane are frequently called on to help Lydia and Wickham with their insoluble financial problems. Elizabeth, Darcy, and his sister Georgiana live amicably at Pemberley. Caroline Bingley is reconciled to her brother's marriage, primarily because of her snobbish desire to be invited to Pemberley frequently. Even Lady Catherine is eventually convinced to permit a reconciliation with her nephew. Elizabeth and Darcy live happily ever after, especially grateful to the Gardiners, "who had been the means of uniting them."

COMMENTARY: This last chapter provides the denouement, removing all the main and subsidiary actors from the stage. It is the end of the Cinderella myth, showing how the prince finally carried off the wallflower to his palace far away. The most interesting aspect of this denouement is that Jane Austen emphasizes the social, rather than the personal, happiness resulting from the marriage: we do not see Elizabeth and Darcy surrounded by their children in a cozy cottage, we see them in their continuing relations with other people. Their marriage takes its place in a larger, overall harmony composed of numerous people and many other marriages.

COMMENTARY: Volume III   The third volume provides most of the falling action of *Pride and Prejudice*. After the senseless separation, Darcy and Elizabeth are gradually brought together. The turn toward each other had begun in Volume II, with the letter from Darcy and Elizabeth's favorable reaction to it. In Volume III, their convergence is continued and accelerated, largely because of two major events.

The first event is Elizabeth's visit to Pemberley with the Gardiners. Here Elizabeth gets her first clear insight into Darcy's character, first through the testimony of his retainers (such as Mrs. Reynolds), then through the meeting with Darcy. The high praise which she hears is absolutely incompatible with her own experience of Darcy, and she begins to modify her views. Then she gets to see Darcy in his own lair, away from strangers, free to act as he wishes. He turns out be a very civil, decent person. Her eyes are now opened and she can admit that she loves him. She can say to Jane later (Ch. 59) that she began to love him "from my first seeing his beautiful grounds at Pemberley." This statement is playful, but degrees of truth lie in it. In the last chapter, we hear that they are both grateful to the Gardiners for "bringing her into Derbyshire."

The second event seems to work in the opposite direction: Wickham's elopement with Lydia. On the surface it *appears* to destroy all chances for the union of Darcy and Elizabeth; actually it enables Darcy to prove his true worth. For awhile their reconciliation is halted, but they are soon moving to the happy ending in which they are married.

CRITICAL ANALYSIS

When we discuss any work of art, we profit as much by noticing what it is *not* about as well as what it *is* about. With no other artist is this negative approach so profitable as Jane Austen; this is shown by the fact that any discussion of her novels seems inevitably to begin with her limitations, or the omissions of her art. Without implying her inferiority to other novelists, we may begin our discussion by summing up some of the things not found in *Pride and Prejudice* and her other novels.

What are some of the things that we have not found in *Pride and Prejudice?* Death, for one thing, and any of the grander, metaphysical experiences of life. She does not show us any of the great agonies of human experience, or the darker side of life. We see nothing of hunger, poverty, misery; her novels do not deal with any of the grand passions or terrible vices one finds in life; we see nothing of God, and very little of a spiritual sphere of experience.

We see only a limited range of human society, too. Most of her people are of the kind she knew intimately—the landed gentry, the upper classes, the lower edge of the nobility, the lower clergy, the officer corps of the military. As we have noticed before (see *Background*) her novels exclude the lower classes, not only the industrial masses of the big cities, but also the agricultural laborers who must have been numerous around Meryton and Longbourn. We do not see the political dimensions of the situation; the people of Meryton seem oblivious to the political affairs disturbing London and the world, and have no political interests of a local kind.

Jane Austen's novels are curiously devoid of any reference to nature itself. It is one of the ironies of English literary history that at a time when the English romantic writers—Wordsworth, Coleridge, Byron, Shelly, Keats and others—were discovering external nature, Jane Austen manages to keep her characters imprisoned indoors, very much the way the eighteenth-century writers did. Hence we have very few passages of description, especially of natural setting. The only description of "nature" in *Pride and Prejudice* is the description of Pemberley (Ch. 43), and it is brief and fairly generalized. The only lesson Elizabeth derives from this natural beauty is "that to be mistress of Pemberley might be something!" "The proper study of mankind is man," Jane would say with Alexander Pope.

And the "man" that she observes would be a man indoors, away from nature, of a special kind. She creates characters who are devoid of any strong passions, the violent emotions which one finds in the fictional creations of Dickens, Dostoyevsky, and other 19th century novelists. Her people are all rather reasonable social creatures, occasionally disturbed and upset, but not given to frenzies, displays of irrationality, violent psychological conflicts, or volcanic furies. This does not mean that they are wooden, unemotional puppets: see Elizabeth's reaction to Darcy's letter (Ch. 36) or her reaction to the elopement (Ch. 46) when she "burst into tears." Still, when these are admitted, any reader with Dostoyevskyan tastes will be disappointed by the calmness of her characters, including those in love.

So far, we have been discussing only the elements lacking in her art, and the casual reader may well wonder how a novel may still be great if so much is missing. This is a question which the Janeites must answer periodically, for there are critics who find her works shallow, restricted, narrow. She herself admitted her limitations, saying that "3 or 4 Families in a Country Village is the very thing to work upon." Charlotte Bronte called Jane Austen's art a "Chinese fidelity, a miniature delicacy in the painting," and disapproved. From the beginning Jane Austen had her defenders, however. Sir Walter Scott envied her, saying in his diary, "The big Bow-Wow strain I can do myself like any now going; but the exquisite touch which renders common-place things and characters interesting from the truth of the description and the sentiment is denied me." The intelligent reader is brought face-to-face with the recurring dilemma of novel criticism: Fielding or Richardson? Scott or Austen? Thomas Wolfe or Hemingway? One may circumvent the dilemma by asking another question: is it not possible to like both kinds of novel and reject neither?

Plot

Pride and Prejudice is an excellent example of Jane Austen's art; some have even called it the most typical of her novels. Here, for example, is the typical Austen plot: an eligible bachelor comes to a small country village where an unmarried girl lives, and the problem of the novel is to get the two married in spite of certain obstacles in their path. In *Pride and Prejudice* this "typical plot" is extended by the fact that there are *two* young ladies in a small village being courted by two bachelors.

The obstacles to the marriages of these two couples are both external and internal. The external obstacles are numerous. First, there is the economic status of the Bennet family; the two bachelors must be willing to accept the disadvantages of marrying into a lower class. Then there are the rather vulgar members of the Bennet family, especially Mrs. Bennet, who do their worst to drive off these would-be husbands. The elopement of Lydia and Wickham is a manifestation of the vulgarity out of which Elizabeth and Jane have come, and they rightly fear the danger of being abandoned by their suitors. A melodramatic obstacle is provided by the stratagems of Darcy and Caroline, who for awhile do their best to keep Bingley from Jane. Caroline also does her best to halt Darcy's growing interest in Elizabeth.

More important, perhaps, than these external antagonists are the internal obstacles in each of the major characters. Darcy is too haughty and outwardly repellent, and deceives others by his appearance; he is proud and officious in hindering the progress of Bingley's affair with Jane. Elizabeth is too quick to judge others and immediately develops a prejudice against Darcy. Bingley and Jane are both too malleable, and hence have their love affair manipulated by others.

As all of these obstacles are overcome—especially Darcy's pride and Elizabeth's prejudice—the way is made clear for their marriages. The novel pleases us because of our sense of obstacles being met and overcome, and the triumph we share with people we like. Once again the Cinderella myth is completed and we are satisfied.

Aside from this very basic pleasure we have in reading the happy ending, we experience the esthetic pleasure of watching the author organize her plot. Mary Lascelles has described the plot as a series of diverging and converging lines:[1]

Elizabeth
Darcy

Shortly after they meet, Elizabeth and Darcy begin to diverge because of their "pride" and "prejudice." Most of this movement is due to Elizabeth because Darcy quickly realizes that he should find some concord with this fascinating girl. But Elizabeth is obdurate: secretly her feelings are wounded by his insulting manner at the dance; she feels that Darcy has held Bingley a virtual prisoner in London, away from Jane. The story of Wickham seems to prove that Darcy is something of a tyrant; and he is a relative of Lady Catherine de Bourgh, whom Elizabeth learns to detest without difficulty. The movement of Darcy and Elizabeth away from each other continues to some maximum point when the lines begin to converge.

What this point is, is a matter of some dispute among readers. Some critics take Elizabeth's explanation, that she began to love Darcy at Pemberley; this is especially appealing to those critics who emphasize the economic theme of the book. The real turn of the book, however, is Elizabeth's receiving of the letter from Darcy. First, it indicates the lengths to which Darcy will go to win Elizabeth since he humbles himself before her immediately after the scene in which she insults him. Second, it initiates Elizabeth's revaluation of all the data she has already, including the relations between Jane and Bingley, and Wickham's story. The revaluation begun by the letter—although it is not completed until their meeting at Pemberley—does shift the balance in her mind; she may continue for awhile to reject the notion of marrying Darcy, but she is now at least able to recognize the good qualities of the man.

Once the lines begin to converge, their progess is not perfect. Rather at one point the convergence is temporarily halted,

[1] *Jane Austen and Her Art* (Oxford, 1939), p. 160.

with the elopement of Lydia and Wickham. The stigma of the Bennet family seems too dark to ever be removed and the hopes of Jane and Elizabeth seem permanently shattered. However, Darcy is secretly at work attempting to rectify matters, and it is only a matter of time before the two couples are united.

The clarity, neatness, simplicity, and symmetry of the plot movement is one of the most pleasing features of the novel. One is tempted to visualize the movements of dancers in a minuet, which (significantly for our discussion of theme, below) takes part of its beauty from the overall organization of many dancers.

As for symmetry, notice that the plot moves through a series of balancing events or incidents. The novel is divided into three parts, the first and last balanced against each other: Part I occurs largely at Longbourn and Netherfield Park; Part II is at Rosings Park; Part III is at Pemberley, then returns to Longbourn. Numerous balancing events occur at various points in the novel. There are two arrivals of Bingley and Darcy; one is at the beginning and occurs in an atmosphere of optimism, the second is near the end and is rather gloomy. There is a series of social affairs opening the novel—the parties and balls— and another series, the marriages, close the novel. There are two surprise marriages, Charlotte's near the beginning and Lydia's near the end. In the beginning Darcy finds himself an alien in strange surroundings; near the end—at Hunsford and at Pemberley—Elizabeth is the stranger who is made uncomfortable in new surroundings. Near the beginning Darcy interferes in Jane's love affair; near the end he interferes in Lydia's, this time with more satisfactory results. Elizabeth has two interviews with Lady Catherine de Bourgh, first at Rosings Park, then at Longbourn. Through these balanced events, and many others like them, Jane Austen achieves a pleasingly symmetrical plot.

What cannot be summarized in this discussion of plot is how each event, each slight incident, each conversation, each speech in a Jane Austen novel is indispensable to the plot. (See *Additional Discussion*, below.) By means of the very limitations we have recognized in her art—the three to four families, the lack of grand incidents, the limitations of her fictional characterizations—Jane Austen is able to articulate all the parts of her novel, down to the slightest detail. Nothing is missing here, and nothing is wasted. It is for her ability to create a perfect unity in her novel that she is respected by the critics and her fellow novelists.

Themes

As for her subject matter and themes, they are neither too complex nor very profound; they are serious, however, and she has something important to say.

Her main subject is courtship and marriage. There are seven marriages in *Pride and Prejudice*, all of them undoubtedly intended to reveal first of all the requirements of a "good" and "bad" marriage. Discounting the Lucases and the Gardiners, what do the five important marriages show?

Obviously, one example of a bad marriage, in Jane Austen's view, is the marriage based on economics, such as that contracted by Mr. Collins and Charlotte Lucas. As a result of Charlotte's need for financial security, she is willing to destroy her own life by linking herself to a pompous ass. In Jane Austen's novels we see the pressures of the economic system being exerted against the young girl. In her time, an unmarried woman was doomed to the unhappy life of caring for someone else's children —as Jane Austen did herself. Otherwise there were no outlets for women in industry, commerce, business, or education. The female was indeed one of the most pitiful victims of the economic system. The novels of Jane Austen—especially *Pride and Prejudice*— dramatize the economic inequality of women, showing how women had to marry undesirable mates in order to gain some financial security. It is no exaggeration to see the system as another form of prostitution.

The second kind of "bad" marriage is the marriage based on such superficial qualities as sex, appearance, good looks, and youthful vivacity. The most obvious example of this is the runaway marriage of Lydia and Wickham, which ends in a kind of mutual tolerance. Wickham often leaves Lydia alone while he cavorts in London, and both are dependent on Elizabeth and Jane for financial support. The sexual attraction between them, once so strong, has apparently disappeared.

A less obvious example of this kind of marriage is that between Mr. and Mrs. Bennet. Undoubtedly they were once attracted to each other very much as Lydia and Wickham were. Even at this late date, Mrs. Bennet is similar to Lydia in her silliness and shallowness (Ch. 41), and it is no accident that Mr. Bennet calls Wickham his "favourite son-in-law." If Lydia's marriage to Wickham ends in a kind of coarseness, that of the Bennets ends in mutual forbearance; Mr. Bennet is in general retreat and isolation, and Mrs. Bennet is a completely disorganized woman. The failure of their marriage is best indicated by the daughters they have raised.

The two examples of "good" marriages are, of course, those of Jane and Elizabeth. Elizabeth's analysis of the happy ending of Jane and Bingley applies even more to herself and Darcy; indeed it sums up one of the main purposes of the novel:

> Elizabeth really believed all Bingley's expectations of felicity to be *rationally* founded, because they had for basis the excellent *understanding* and super-excellent disposition of Jane, and a general similarity of feeling and taste between her and himself.
>
> (Ch. 55)

The italics indicate the values which Jane Austen emphasizes through her novels. One theme of the novel is that hasty marriages like that of Lydia and Wickham quickly cool and inevitably lead to unhappiness; the marriages which are based on a calm judgment and are well-considered beforehand are more apt to survive. At first, Elizabeth and Darcy were distant and prejudiced against each other; the series of events which they experienced helped them to understand each other, and their marriage will be stable because of this mutual experience and understanding.

This theme of fully knowing one's mate before marrying is a small part of a larger theme, that of distinguishing appearance from reality. "What is true?" is a theme handled by every great writer, including Jane Austen. We have seen throughout our discussion how everyone in the book is deceived on some point or another, usually because of trust in appearances. To list all of the examples would be tedious, but we may point to a few noteworthy events to illustrate the theme: Wickham's deception of Meryton, including Elizabeth, concerning his character and his dealings with Darcy; Darcy's repellent character at the beginning of the novel; Lady Catherine's underestimation of Eliazbeth, both when Elizabeth visits Rosings and when Lady Catherine visits Longbourn; Mr. and Mrs. Bennet's failure to recognize that Elizabeth was in love with Darcy until it had been announced to them; Darcy's inability to see that Jane was really in love with Bingley; Elizabeth's failure to see Charlotte's desire for a husband; Mr. Collins' unwillingness to see Elizabeth's honesty when she rejects him. We have also mentioned that the dialogue often makes the intended meaning obscure, both to the characters listening and to the reader. Only at the end of the book is everything made clear, to characters and reader alike, and only then does all the "reality" appear as it really is.

Finally, a theme which needs to be stressed is the theme of the organic unity of society. Jane Austen, as we have said, reflects the 18th century view that man is primarily a social animal and has responsibilities to the rest of society. The individual must subordinate his feelings and needs to the larger purposes of the society of which he is a part.

Even love is to be interpreted as less an individual act than a social act: it occurs at the will of the society, according to its laws, and it will affect all the members of society. Society is a web of personal relations, most readily seen in the network of relationships inside the family. Love and marriage are first of all important to members of the immediate families, but their influence spreads out like ripples in a pond to touch distant members of the family, and finally the society itself. The elopement of Wickham and Lydia, passionate and irresponsible, is an example of how other lives may be ruined by the selfish acts of the individual: had the marriage not been immediately arranged by members of the families concerned (Mr. Gardiner for the Bennets, and Darcy for Wickham), the happiness of Jane and Elizabeth would have been permanently jeopardized. We are also led to assume that even Darcy would have been permanently scarred by the scandal, suspecting as he did that somehow he was responsible for Wickham. Conversely, the marriages which end the book are shown in the context of the families concerned; we are told as much about Lydia and Wickham, Mr. and Mrs. Bennet, Georgiana Darcy, Caroline Bingley, and Lady Catherine as we are of Jane and Bingley, Elizabeth and Darcy. The marriages contracted by these four bring happiness and stability to everyone, not simply to themselves.

Paradoxically, Jane Austen does not go so far as to say that family considerations should be all-important. Darcy and Elizabeth marry in spite of his family obligations, which are pressed on him by Lady Catherine. Jane Austen avoids the charge of inconsistency by concealing the discussion between Lady Catherine and Darcy; in any case, we can imagine that however "logical" Lady Catherine's arguments, they will somehow be invalidated by her tactlessness and dictatorial manner.

Darcy's decision to marry Elizabeth thus not only flies in the face of convention, but undermines any abstract philosophical attitude toward marriage which one may read into Jane Austen's novel. In short, Jane Austen's world is much more complex than some readers and critics have claimed. She does not give the reader simplistic interpretations of life: she does not say to marry only for love, or only for family, or only for the good of society. She is not a philosopher but an artist who gives us particular individuals working under specific kinds of circumstances. By giving us a sense of life in all of its aspects, her novels achieve the complexity and intricacy of great art.

Dialogue

Jane Austen's use of dialogue is really a reflection of her 18th century background, for it shows that she is less interested in the physical appearance of any of her characters than she is in the *essential* qualities which make up their inner nature. In spite of this concern with the inner nature, however, Jane Austen does not resort to the technique of *analysis;* only rarely does she resort to recording the interior conflicts of her people. Least of all is she interested in the delicate movements of the unconscious or subconscious mind, the impressions, the mental sensations which the Freudian age finds so fascinating.

Being an Augustan, she is interested in man in society, man as a social animal. And man in society is primarily a talking creature, a creature engaged in dialogue. Hence it is no surprise to find that most of her characterization is accomplished through dialogue. In fact, she is generally regarded as a model for all novelists interested in the writing of excellent conversation.

This does not mean simply that she gives the modern reader some idea of what 18th century drawing-room conversation was like, or what two young people talked about in those days. More important, her dialogue is the main vehicle for the revelation of character; the people in her novels reveal themselves simply, accurately, and completely whenever they speak. What an individual says is often pregnant with other meanings which the reader must be alert to catch. Although some critics find Jane Austen's novels superficial, the complexity and undercurrents of her dialogue make her novels among the most difficult to be read *properly*. A reader should not be contented with a single reading of the novel; the novel once read, should be re-read in order to appreciate the many nuances and subtleties of the conversation. One must add that a guidebook can assist but cannot be any meaningful substitute for a sensitive and careful reading.

Some examples of her mastery of dialogue might be useful. In Chapter 6, Charlotte Lucas' discussion of Jane's "guarded character" seems to be innocent enough, the simple advice of a close friend. Later, however, the reader realizes how that conversation throws light on Charlotte's own character, explaining somewhat her hasty acceptance of marriage, and showing her to be as anxious about marriage as she imagined Jane to be. Furthermore, when Darcy later tells Elizabeth that Jane had not "appeared" to be in love with Bingley, Elizabeth recalls Charlotte's advice. It suggests to her that Darcy is not alone, that he may have been correct in doubting Jane's sincerity, and that Elizabeth's values need readjusting. The innocuous discussion with Charlotte, then, is an integral part of the characterization and the movement of the plot.

Another example: shortly after they meet, Darcy is growing to like Elizabeth, but Elizabeth already distrusts, even dislikes Darcy. He attempts to mollify her one evening at Netherfield (Ch. 10). When Caroline Bingley sits down at the piano, Darcy approaches Elizabeth and asks:

> "Do you feel a great inclination, Miss Bennet, to
> seize such an opportunity of dancing a reel?"

This seems to be an innocent question. But not to a person who distrusts the questioner. In the 18th century, the reel was a rather "countrified" dance, most often done in the rural areas, and not exactly acceptable in the best salons of London. Elizabeth is immediately offended then at the suggestion that she is a country girl given to such pastimes, or preferences in dancing. Furthermore, the words "great inclination" suggest that Elizabeth is given to impulsive behavior, or uncivilized, even barbarous activities. She therefore pauses:

> She smiled but made no answer. He repeated the question, with some surprise at her silence.

Elizabeth is arming herself for an answer to a question she thinks is doubly insulting. Darcy must repeat the question and is of course surprised, since he is only being sociable. She finally answers:

> "Oh," said she, "I heard you before, but I could not immediately determine what to say in reply. You wanted me, I know, to say "Yes," that you might have the pleasure of despising my taste; but I always delight in overthrowing those kind of schemes and cheating a person of their premeditated contempt. I have therefore made up my mind to tell you that I do not want to dance a reel at all —and now despise me if you dare."

Elizabeth reveals the extent of her animus against Darcy, who is shocked by her reply. Not only does she refuse his request; she accuses him of having a "premeditated contempt" for her; he has deliberately schemed to make a fool of her by showing what a despicable taste she has—for reel, and other amusements indulged in by country bumpkins. She triumphantly adds, "despise me if you dare." That is: "You cannot despise me for dancing a reel, so you can try to despise me for refusing to dance with you and seeing through your little game. I have beaten you, Mr. Darcy."

To which Mr. Darcy replies with an equally pregnant, "Indeed, I do not dare." The reader must decide on the tone in which this is said. A prejudiced reader might conclude that the tone is contemptuous, as a kind of defense against this girl's insult. One may detect a matter-of-fact tone, indicating a kind of gallantry, as Elizabeth does; Darcy may be simply retiring coldly to his corner rather than indulging in further repartee, or is this a tone of true affection or at least growing affection? The next paragraph suggests that Darcy is in "some danger"—that is, danger of falling in love. "Indeed, I do not dare" may simply mean, "I have been beaten now, but you are such an attractive woman that I do not care to jeopardize my chances with you any more than I have done already with this slight misunderstanding. I shall live to fight another day."

The tones of Darcy's statement range from outright antagonism to veiled affection. This is just one example of the complexity inherent in Jane Austen's dialogue. It reveals that the reader must play an active part in reading the novel, interpreting clues, relating parts of the novel together, noticing nuances of tone and meaning. The reader who assumes that all of Jane Austen's novel is superficial misses half the pleasure and most of the artistry.

CHARACTER ANALYSIS

Elizabeth   Jane Austen said of Elizabeth, the second daugh-
Bennet   ter, that "I think her as delightful a creature as
ever appeared in print, and how I shall be able to tolerate those
who do not like *her* at least I do not know." (Letter to Cassandra,
Jan. 1813). Generations of readers have vindicated her estimate;
Robert Louis Stevenson was so enthusiastic about Elizabeth that
whenever she spoke he wanted to "go down on his knees."

One reason for this strong admiration is that she is a complex creation. We find her fascinating because there are several
sides to her.

For most readers she appeals because in her character
there is a combined softness and hardness. She is fairly attractive
(as Darcy comes to admit), is receptive to the hero, and genu-
inely desirable as a woman. But there is a masculine strength in
her, a clarity of vision, a directness of purpose that raises her
above the run-of-the-mill heroine. Above all, she has good sense.
Throughout the novel, she is able to direct Jane, raise her spirits,
tell her how to win Bingley. She has enough self-command not to
be intimidated by the mighty—including Darcy and Lady Catherine. She can see beneath the surfaces of life's pomp and circum-
stance, and realize that they mean very little; she knows that
human integrity and happiness mean more than the comforts and
security of rank and prestige. She is understanding of the elements of the human personality; she knows all the foibles, the
distortions, the exaggerations. Aware that people like Caroline
and Lady Catherine can ruin the lives of others, she is quick to
dissect and deflate the fatuous, the stupid, the pretentious, and
the vicious.

Although these masculine qualities in her make her appear
rather eccentric, even repellent, to those first meeting her, they
account for part of the appeal she exerts on the female reader.
Her appeal to the male reader lies in the other direction: she
retains enough of her feminine "softness" to keep her human. She
is not completely "masculine" or "rational"—as perhaps Mary is—
and is thus not dehumanized. She is capable of certain feminine

frailties and weakesses; she brings out in Darcy, and in the male reader, the protective instinct which the true female does.

She errs especially in analyzing three persons who are close to her: Charlotte, Wickham, and Darcy. There is no one single reason for her failure here. One is tempted to say that generally it is her vanity which leads Elizabeth astray, making her fallible, human, and finally sympathetic: the male reader sees something of the eternal female in her, and loves her. Her dislike of Darcy stems from one event: his refusal to dance with her because she is not attractive enough. Her trust in Wickham, utterly illogical, is because he is an eligible bachelor who chooses to make conversation with her rather than with anyone else in the party of attractive women present; and this conversation occurs shortly after the insulting incident with Darcy. Her inability to understand Charlotte is a result of Elizabeth's assumption that everyone—and especially her best friend—is like her and must therefore be ambitious for the same things; Charlotte's quick acceptance of Collins' proposal is a direct affront to Elizabeth's set of standards.

This overweening vanity of Elizabeth's leads one to conclude that it is not Darcy alone who is guilty of "pride." Indeed, Elizabeth's main problem may be her "vanity" or "pride" rather than her "prejudice." Out of that vanity grows her prejudice, and it is only when her vanity is destroyed (when she sees her own fallibility) that the prejudice evaporates. In the process, she wins the affections of every reader.

Jane Bennet
Jane is the eldest daughter, hence *Miss* Bennet. She is the most attractive (physically) of the Bennet daughters, and very desirable to impressionable bachelors like Bingley. Some critics have estimated Jane as equal in importance to Elizabeth, but she is better seen as a foil to Elizabeth. She is "perfect" in only a superficial way; that is, she surpasses Elizabeth in outward appearance, but she has none of the wisdom or strength of character that Elizabeth has. Jane Austen does not bother to develop Jane Bennet's character fully: she is virtually absent through the middle portion of the book, and she is portrayed constantly as a character who reacts, rather than acts.

Even the love affair between Jane and Bingley is less a matter of their own determination than a by-product of Elizabeth and Darcy's affair. Jane and Bingley are gentle, naive, malleable souls who are subject to the decisions and strong wills of others around them. They will be happy together because they are so well suited for each other. But they will need the protection of someone more worldly, more practical—someone like Darcy and Elizabeth.

Mary   Mary, the third daughter, is a complete carica-
Bennet   ture of the unsocial, bookish black-sheep. Most critics agree that she is the failure in the book (if there is one) because she is so unbelievable. Actually, she is part of Jane Austen's design in the book, serving to balance the non-intellectual and scatter-brained Lydia and Kitty. For those at all familiar with sociology, she is entirely credible as a part of the normal pattern that one discovers in families, and is thus more realistic than the critics say. Unable to establish normal relations with people around her, she retreats into her world of books and the pianoforte; her communications with her family are limited to platitudes, stock responses, and moralizing.

Lydia and   Lydia is the youngest daughter; Kitty is two years
Kitty Bennet   older than Lydia. Both are flirtatious man-hunters, their only interest in men—especially men in uniform. In order to win a husband, they will gladly sacrifice the happiness of those around them. They have no values and no sense of responsibility; they are utterly devoted to a life of dancing, dresses, hats, gossip, and flirtations. They are as oversexed and extroverted as their sister Mary is overintellectual and introverted.

Lydia's brainlessness is made clearer due to the larger role she plays in the novel, but Kitty would have been capable of exactly the same stupidity. It is simply a matter of chance that Lydia is offered the trip to Brighton and therefore wins the booby prize: namely, Wickham. Her marriage to Wickham is an untidy, unstable mess that reflects the inner natures of both.

Mrs. Bennet   A foolish woman, given to silly talk, and obsessed with a single idea: getting her daughters married. That obsession is understandable, however, for her husband has abdicated his role as the family guide. Her own youth was probably not unlike her daughter Lydia's: that is, she was probably a pretty, shallow, flirtatious thing who managed to snare the eligible Mr. Bennet. She is quickly taken with Wickham, and still shows a fondness for uniforms in general. Naturally, she fails utterly to see the virtues in her daughter Elizabeth and Darcy.

Mr. Bennet A man gifted with intelligence, knowledge, wit, and the power to detach himself from the frenzied problems of his family. He is able to see the foolishness surrounding him; he does not see that he is a cause of much of it because of his failure as a father. The book moves in the direction of this relf-realization. The family of which he is the supposed head ends with two definite losses (Mary and Lydia, representing opposite extremes); two uncertainties (Jane and Kitty, both of whom must grow in wisdom in the future); and one success, Elizabeth. Though he acquires an understanding of his own responsibility for the failures of his children, he lapses into indifference at the end of the novel. In spite of his virtues, then, Mr. Bennet is Jane Austen's example of a weak father.

Charles Bingley Bingley is a rather wooden, flat character. Good-looking, mannerly, friendly, easy in society, he has little depth. He recognizes that he has little strength of character. His love affair with Jane progresses fairly smoothly, with no realization on his part of the turmoil he is causing. He agrees with Darcy that he has been easily led, and is given to changing his interests from moment to moment. He can love Jane, abandon her, rediscover her as easily as he abandons or rediscovers the joys of fox-hunting, or of going to the theater. With Jane he will have a simple, uncomplicated, and bland marriage.

Fitzwilliam Darcy Critical opinion on Darcy is divided. The main question is: is he credible or not? Is it likely that a character so "proud" in the first half of the book should suddenly become a sympathetic "hero" in the second half? Or is this change simply a result of our having misread Darcy's character along with Elizabeth? Some critics answer that Darcy is a very convincing characterization and all of a piece. For others, Darcy is one of Jane Austen's most serious failures. They attribute this to her age, saying that the novelist worked on it when she was only 21 or 22 years old, hence was not acquainted with the social world. Others say that Jane Austen is generally weak in drawing male characters, that she is vague when dealing with them, for example, never having any scene in which a woman is not present.

Although such arguments are probably irreconcilable, and depend ultimately on each reader's personal reaction, we may point out some unarguable points. First, Darcy does indeed show "pride" at the beginning of the book; he *does* speak carelessly and insultingly within Elizabeth's hearing, and deserves her coldness. For the reader, there is a problem whether this "pride" and this "carelessness" are at all excused under the conditions: he has just made a long trip; he is in strange company at a large ball; he is naturally awkward in company, showing a shyness that seems to run in the family. (Darcy reminds us of stories told of Lord Byron, who acquired a reputation for being sinister, melancholy, and mysterious, when he was actually only bashful, partly because of a lame foot!)

The argument over Darcy's change of character is insoluble mainly because of a technical feature of the novel: the point of view. For most of the book—and especially the first few chapters—the reader is kept on the outside of Darcy. The novelist does not show us what he is thinking; nor does she analyze him, to guide our responses in a sympathetic way. Rather we see him only from Elizabeth's point of view, and that point of view is, after all, prejudiced. No matter how much we discuss or seem to prove with our evidence, most of that evidence is irreducibly Elizabeth's.

As the book proceeds, we come to discover the truth about Darcy. We see that he is superior to Bingley as a suitor for the heroine. He is more complex, sensitive, and intelligent than the other males in the story. He shares with Elizabeth certain mature qualities: he is as contemptuous as she of family concerns, social ceremonies, and external appearances. Her originality and individualism appeal to him because of the same qualities in him. He and she agree that they do not perform well for others.

Whatever we conclude about Darcy, his faults are certainly minor. It is interesting to note, also, something that is too often overlooked: we very quickly discover what Darcy is really like, since he begins to turn his attentions to Elizabeth by Chapter 6. The astute reader is not misled, as Elizabeth is, about

Darcy's true feelings, and so the change that comes with his letter seems less extreme and less incomprehensible.

George
Wickham
He is the scoundrel and villain of the novel. Most of his energies are directed toward two ends: concealing his true character from those around him, and winning a wife with money. He tries for Elizabeth first but surrenders her when a better prospect, Miss King, appears. He is apparently abandoned by her. His scheme to marry Lydia is little better than blackmail; he knows that the Bennet family will pay a bribe to get Lydia married. Wickham achieves, through a kind of alley-cat cleverness, what he has always wanted.

He is not simply a pasteboard villain, however; he is handsome, charming, and ingenious. He had deceived the old Mr. Darcy; not even Mr. Bennet can find him permanently repulsive; and Elizabeth calls him the "most agreeable man I ever saw," thinking for awhile that she might marry him. Thus Wickham has some real assets, including the charm and wit that often accompany the detestable qualities in a scoundrel.

William
Collins
The immortal fool and one of the great comic creatures of English literature. He is a clergyman in the Church of England; specifically he is the rector (or parson) of a small country parsonage called Hunsford. This means that he should provide the spiritual services for the nearby villagers and farmers, and for the wealthy gentry like Lady Catherine de Bourgh, owner of the great estate. Unfortunately, like many other clergymen in the Church of England during this period, Mr. Collins is not a very good pastor for his sheep. The Church of England had itself lost much of its spiritual power in the late 18th century as a result of certain economic and political conditions. The Church had, for one thing, become a haven for some incompetent men who could not make a living elsewhere; for example, many younger men who could not afford to go to the Universities or who could not depend on any inheritance from their fathers became clergymen. (A good example of this is Wickham, who is plainly unsuited for such a life!) Once these incompetents were assigned their "livings" (posts or positions), they settled down into a kind of irresponsible lethargy.

Mr. Collins shows us what this life could be like. He is a young man grown old before his time, already comfortably set-

tled in the grooves of polite thinking and acting. Being a churchman has not spiritualized Mr. Collins in the least; in fact, he is a
very worldly rector, completely engrossed by such matters as social rank, prestige, position, family connections, and money. Far
from being a dedicated Christian, he is a snob and a toady. He is
completely dominated by Lady Catherine, who dictates to him
the policies of Hunsford Parsonage and the main goals of Mr.
Collins' personal life. Morally empty, pompous, and conceited,
he amuses us constantly, and we cannot forget him.

QUESTIONS AND ANSWERS

1. Pride and Prejudice *was originally entitled* First Impressions. *Defend the change in the title.*

Even a cursory reading of the novel shows us that the book is not only about first impressions. The first impressions which the characters get of each other take up only the first few chapters; after that the novel is concerned primarily with the *effects* of those impressions on the characters. Furthermore, the story is not only about first impressions, that is the prejudices of the characters. The story is equally about the faults of people like Darcy, who *are* proud at the beginning, and people like Wickham who *do* deceive others purposely. The fault then does not lie only with Elizabeth, who misapprehended both of them at first. The novel is as much about Darcy's change of attitudes as it is about Elizabeth's correction of her first impressions. Hence, *Pride and Prejudice* is the better title; defend this position at length with careful evaluation of each character and each character inter-relationship.

2. *Discuss Jane Austen's use of scenery.*

One may pay attention to the scenery one finds in the novel, the descriptive passages concerned with setting, and say something about Jane Austen's values. Draw some conclusions about her main interests: for her, as for most Augustans, "the proper study of mankind is man" and not nature, or physical setting. The setting in her novels is generally only backdrop. When she does describe (as in Pemberley section, Ch. 43), it is usually only in general terms. One may draw conclusions from that quality, concluding that the specific details of nature did not interest her.

3. (*If a novel by Sir Walter Scott has been read, a question may be asked in which the two novels are to be contrasted.*) *Contrast the plots of the two novelists.*

Jane Austen's plots are usually brief, uninvolved, uncomplicated. They do not usually include physical action, certainly not violent, physical action. Subplots are kept to a minimum; number of protagonists and antagonists is very small. The conflicts are basically moral, intellectual, and internal. The stories are usually completed within a relatively brief time, with a minimum of complications, and through a clear series of events.

Scott's plots are just the opposite. They are often long and quite complicated, usually involving mysterious disguises, schemes, tricks. They are often dependent on physical action, often quite violent (e.g., the siege in *Ivanhoe*). There are often subplots—sometimes more than one to a novel—and the number of characters is large. The conflicts are moral too, but they often are resolved by some physical action. The novels of Scott often cover years, and deal with generations in the same family.

4. *Contrast the characters of Jane Austen and Sir Walter Scott.*

Jane Austen's characters are usually from the middle, upper-middle, or lower-upper classes; she is interested in the best in society, who are often intellectual, sensitive people. Her main emphasis is the social and moral problems they meet with.

Sir Walter Scott's main characters are usually lower class, or lower middle class, although he often deals with great historical events in which real, historical personages play a part. (See George Lukac's *The Historical Novel*.) These characters are presented physically and emotionally, rather than intellectually. They are often concerned with personal, moral dilemmas, rather than with problems involving social issues. They often answer their personal dilemmas by some physical activity (e.g., Jeannie Deans walks from Scotland to London in *The Heart of Midlothian* to save her sister.).

5. *Contrast the kinds of moods used in the novels of Jane Austen and Sir Walter Scott.*

In the novels of Jane Austen, the atmosphere is intellectual, cold, and unemotional, at least on the surface. The social surface is undisturbed, although there may be violent emotions

concealed beneath the play of words. The main action of the
novel is the exchange of opinions, ideas, attitudes; the mood is
kept relatively free of emotional charge.

In Scott, the emotion is obvious, strong, often overwhelm-
ing. The novel often involves great emotional scenes, full of
drama; the excitement is readily apparent and easily communica-
ted to the reader. Even in the less dramatic scenes, Scott indulges
in evocative description, mood pieces, colorful settings and characters that enliven the atmosphere. All of this makes for a novel
of mood and emotion in contrast to Jane Austen's more decorous,
intellectual novels, where the emotion has to be perceived beneath the surface.

6. *Analyze the importance and effectiveness of the dialogue of
Jane Austen.*

The importance is undoubted and undebatable. Point out
how much of the novel depends on dialogue, in terms of quantity
alone. As for effectiveness, one must first define the term. Dialogue may be effective first in the creation of character. Choose
several examples of dialogue which you felt were particularly
incisive in the characterization: e.g., you might point to the kind
of nonsense spouted by Collins, or the violent flow of words from
Lady Catherine.

Dialogue may also be important and effective because it
is ambiguous, complex, and intellectually satisfying. Dialogue on
the surface soon loses its charm; dialogue with several implica-
tions and emotional connotations provides pleasure for the
reader. Analyze several passages of such dialogue, (e.g., Darcy's
insulting treatment of Caroline Bingley in Ch. 8).

7. *The problem of Darcy's character is a troublesome one. Defend Darcy as a credible character, or show that Jane Austen's
portrayal of Darcy is feeble.*

This book has defended the characterization of Darcy.
Darcy's change of heart is not really a change but a matter of
Elizabeth's final recognition of his true character. If Darcy is
cold and haughty at the beginning of the novel, he is somewhat

justified. Jane Austen takes care to show us that he is naturally shy and awkward in company; furthermore he is somewhat irritated by the unnatural situation of being introduced to numerous people for whom he cares little. His coolness toward Jane is also explained: he has not realized that she was really in love. The problem ultimately boils down to the fact that Elizabeth has misinterpreted him; when her view finally accords with reality, she and the reader come to understand him. The characterization of Darcy is unified, coherent, whole. In fact, the real Darcy—the admiring, loving Darcy—appears very early in the novel.

The other point of view is that Darcy is not a whole, coherent, credible fictional character, but one of Jane Austen's few mistakes. This may be a result of her own situation: as a spinster who was isolated from male company most of her life, she was unable to understand the psychology of a young man. Hence, Darcy appears to be two different people in the novel, showing Jane Austen's inadequate grasp of his personality. He first appears as a cold, brutal snob, then changes into a decent character who will do anything for Elizabeth. The problem is not that some people may change like this; rather it is that we are expected to believe that he made the change so easily and rapidly. The coldness of Darcy at the beginning simply does not balance with his warmth in the second half. The excuse that he was naturally shy and awkward in company is especially a weak one, since it does not explain his interference in Bingley's affairs. In any case, it is poor strategy for the art of the novel, since the reader is asked suddenly to accept a new Darcy who is not shy, and no longer too proud to be with Elizabeth.

8: *Analyze Elizabeth's character and try to discover the reasons for her popularity. What are the qualities of a "good woman" according to Jane Austen?*

See *Character Analysis* for possible insights. Bring in your own views on her character, perhaps by comparing her with other heroines of popular fiction you have read.

9. *Defend Mary as an important character in the book, and as a credible fictional creature.*

See *Character Analysis*. Show how the Bennet family is ranged on a scale from pure intellect to pure emotion, and how Mary is needed to fill one space to provide a balance to Lydia and Kitty. If you know anything about social psychology, show how her character is a part of the family pattern.

10. *Discuss the theme of appearance vs. reality in the novel.*

See *Critical Analysis* for suggestions.

11. *What are the standards of a good marriage, according to Jane Austen?*

Dicuss all the marriages in the book (see *Comprehensive Summary*), and analyze closely the relationship between Darcy and Elizabeth.

12. *List the obstacles to marriage, and say something about which obstacles Jane Austen considers most serious.*

See *Critical Analysis*. One may divide the obstacles into two types: external and internal, or social and psychological. One may argue about which Jane Austen considers more serious: is the relationship between Darcy and Elizabeth jeopardized more by Elizabeth's dislike of Darcy or by the sudden elopement of Lydia? One may argue the point, since both are serious enough.

13. *During the course of the book, Elizabeth considers the possibility of being married to three men: Collins, Wickham and Darcy. Discuss specifically the advantages each man has as a potential husband, and arrive at some conclusions about Jane Austen's views on the subject of a "good" husband.*

Clearly Wickham offers Elizabeth the advantages of his handsomeness, his attractiveness, his exciting life as an officer: that is, he is all externals. Collins offers the advantages of financial security and social position: he himself is not handsome, and the life he offers is a dull one at Hunsford. Darcy combines both of these, being fairly handsome and desirable, and also being wealthy. More important, however, he has some qualities neither of the two have: good sense, decorum, intelligence, wit, and common sense. For Jane Austen, a combination of good looks and money would be insufficient prerequisites for a husband.

RESEARCH AREAS

As the student is aware, a guidebook can never exhaustively discuss all the elements of a novel; if anything, it can only bring to the surface more questions. The student may now wish to engage in further research to answer these questions in term papers of varying sizes.

Background: Biographical and Historical

1. Influence of Jane Austen's life on the subject matter of the novel.

Read the biographies and letters of Jane Austen. Show how her personal life (her country background, her spinsterhood, her family) is reflected in the materials of the novel.

2. Military background.

Read in the history of the times (especially on the subject of the English army during the period 1795-1820) and clarify the military situation in the novel. Explain such details as the stationing of the regiment at Meryton, its movement to Brighton, its organization. Discuss the nature of an army career for such people as Wickham, and the life he and Lydia can expect to live.

3. Social life in England.

Read some histories of the time (especially social histories such as that by G. M. Trevelyan and A. S. Turberville) for details on the social details of this novel, e.g., the balls, courtship and marriage, family estates, elopements, the position of clergymen in the society and so on.

4. Legal background.

A short paper might be written on the custom of "entailing" an estate, and the exact financial arrangements existing between Collins and the Bennet family. Also bring in the financial arrangements made for Lydia's dowry.

Literary Background

1. A detailed comparison of Jane Austen and Sir Walter Scott.

A number of research papers might be done on this general topic. One may read one, or a number of novels, and write a comparison of the two contemporaries. Or one may limit the paper to a single artistic element—the plot, the scenery, methods of characterization, mood—as revealed in a number of novels. One may also go on to generalize about the nature of popularity from a reading of the novels.

2. A comparison of Jane Austen and Henry Fielding.

The same directions apply here as in the topic involving Scott. Fielding is a favorite subject here because Jane Austen shares some of Fielding's preoccupations and ideas. The comparison should be enlightening on the progress of the novel between 1750 and 1800.

3. Jane Austen and the Augustans.

For a larger paper, read some of the poems of Pope, Swift's *Gulliver's Travels*, the essays of Addison and Steele, the poems and essays of Samuel Johnson. (For reinforcement read such studies of intellectual history as Walter Bate's *From Classic to Romantic*, A. O. Lovejoy's *The Great Chain of Being*, and Leslie Stephen's *History of English Thought in the Eighteenth Century*.) Discuss the degree of similarity between Jane Austen's predecessors and her novels, in ideas, content, subject matter, and style.

4. Jane Austen's place as a "female novelist."

Read some of the other female novelists writing at about Jane Austen's time—for example, Fanny Burney, Anne Radcliffe, Charlotte Smith, Elizabeth Inchbald. Discuss to what extent she is indebted to them, and to what extent she surpasses them as an artist.

Jane Austen's Artistry

(Although not exactly "research topics," the following subjects may still serve as term paper projects.)

1. Plot. Find definitions of "plot" (e.g., in Aristotle) and show how Jane Austen's novel does or does not satisfy the requirements of a "plot." Discuss her contribution to the history of "plot" by showing what kind of incidents, events, organization, she uses in her novel.

2. The importance of the Darcy-Elizabeth plot. Show how everything in the novel, down to the slightest incident, is dependent on the Darcy-Elizabeth plot; include here all the other love affairs, especially the Charlotte Lucas-Collins affair, and the Jane-Bingley affair.

3. Characterization. Discuss the characters of Jane Austen's novels on a spectrum ranging from "good" to "bad," defining first what makes a "bad" character and what makes a "good" character in Jane Austen's view.

4. Characterization: Maturity. Show how "maturity" is the primary virtue for Jane Austen. Define this term as Jane Austen sees it;   then divide the characters into mature and immature characters. Show how the novel is primarily concerned with the important theme of the need to grow into mature wisdom.

5. Characterization: Depth. Analyze closely what Jane Austen tells us about a character and what she conceals from us. What sides of human nature is she least concerned with, and why? Why does she, for example, give us so little of the person's physical description? What does this reveal about her main interests?

6. Setting. Discuss Jane Austen's use of—or neglect of—physical setting. To what extent does she describe the physical setting, and in what terms? Note especially the description of Pemberley, and analyze (Ch. 43).

7. Style: Dialogue. Analyze closely Jane Austen's use of speaking style for characterizing people. Show how the major characters

reveal themselves by the way they talk. Pay attention especially to the following characters: Mr. Collins, Lydia, Lady Catherine, Mrs. Bennet, and Elizabeth. (Acquaint yourself with the elements of style by reading a book like Herbert Read's *English Prose Style*.)

8. Irony. Discuss Jane Austen's use of irony. Acquaint yourself with the definitions of irony (including dramatic irony). Show how the events happen ironically throughout the novel (e.g., the appearance of Mr. Collins, the argument between Elizabeth and Darcy at Hunsford, the news of Lydia's elopement). Show further how Jane Austen uses irony in the speeches of her favorite characters (e.g., Elizabeth), and how her own narration is dependent on irony (e.g., look at the first sentence of the book: how does it show irony by saying the opposite of what it means?).

9. Satire. Can a case be made for *Pride and Prejudice* as satirical? This will involve discussion of the problem of artistic "sincerity." There arises conflict between an evident honesty on Austen's part, portraying aspects of her personal life and personal observation in the novel (see *Background: Biographical.* 1, above), and a possible and frequent reading of the novel whereby all becomes tongue-in-cheek as was the tone of her literary models: Fielding, Pope, Swift, etc. (see *Literary Background*, above, and *The Literary Climate*, above).

BIBLIOGRAPHY

Background: Biographical and Historical

Apperson, G. L. *A Jane Austen Bibliography*. London: Cecil Palmer, 1932. The person, places, books, authors named in her works; also names of her relatives, friends, associates.

Austen, Jane. *Letters to her sister Cassandra and Others*. ed. R. W. Chapman. Two volumes. Oxford: Clarendon Press, 1932.

These letters are often dull, showing the limited scope of her activities and interests. However they are indispensable for they show the "even tenor" of her life. (References to *Pride and Prejudice* in Volume II.)

Austen-Leigh, William and Richard A. *Jane Austen: Her Life and Letters, a Family Record*. London: 1913. The authoritative biography.

Chapman, R. W. *Jane Austen: A Critical Bibliography*. Oxford: Clarendon Press, 1953. Full description of the first editions, translations, and later editions. Has a brief biography, and then an interesting series of statements by famous writers on the subject of Jane Austen.

.... *Jane Austen: Facts and Problems*. Oxford: Clarendon Press, 1950. Presents us with all the materials for knowing her better. Includes a biography (with a good chapter on her "romances") and an interesting reading of her personality. Detailed bibliography and chronology.

Hill, Constance. *Jane Austen: Her Homes and Friends*. New York and London: John Lane, 1902. Many paintings and sketches of the Jane Austen country, family, friends. A simple narration and description of a visit to this area.

Jenkins, Elizabeth. *Jane Austen.* London: Victor Gollancz Ltd., 1939. Still the fullest modern biography; includes some criticism. Highly recommended.

Mitton, Geraldine E. *Jane Austen and her Times.* New York: G. P. Putnam's Sons, and London: Methuen and Co., 1905. More interesting in the digressions on various related subjects—the clergy, traveling, the navy, contemporary writers, fashions.

Critical

Babb, Howard S. *Jane Austen's Novels: the Fabric of Dialogue.* Columbus, Ohio: Ohio State Univ. Press, 1962. A careful analysis of Jane Austen's use of dialogue as indication of the emotions of the characters.

Bailey, John. *Introductions to Jane Austen.* London: Humphrey Milford, 1931. Brief discussions of each novel, and a biography.

Cecil, Lord David. *Jane Austen.* (The Leslie Stephen Lecture, delivered before the University of Cambridge on 1 May 1935.) Cambridge: Cambridge University Press, 1936. A brief appreciation of the novelist by a sensitive reader; emphasizes that the novels are universal because of her ability to create characters. (Reprinted in *Poets and Story-Tellers*, New York; the Macmillan Company, 1949.)

Kaye-Smith, Sheila and G. B. Stern. *Speaking of Jane Austen.* New York and London: Harper and Brothers, Publishers, 1944. Two "Janeites" display their idolatry in a collection of personal essays.

.... *More about Jane Austen.* New York and London: Harper and Brothers, Publishers, 1949. More personal impression by these ardent admirers.

Kennedy, Margaret. *Jane Austen.* Denver: Alan Swallow, 1950. A very brief but dependable treatment of the life and novels.

Lascelles, Mary. *Jane Austen and her Art*. Oxford: Clarendon Press, 1939. The one book to read on Jane Austen. A brief biography followed by very sensible chapters on her reading, her style, her narrative art. Highly recommended.

Mudrick, Marvin. *Jane Austen: Irony as Defense and Discovery*. Princeton, N. J.: Princeton University Press, 1952. Argues that Jane Austen's novels were primarily in rebellion against her society. Overemphasizes the sexual problems raised by Wickham and Darcy.

Southam, B. C. *Jane Austen's Literary Manuscripts*. Oxford: Oxford University Press, 1964. A study of the remaining manuscripts of her works, which do not include the major novels.

Warner, Sylvia Townsend. *Jane Austen, 1775-1817*. London, N.Y., and Toronto: Longmans Green and Co., 1951. Brief biography and sensitive comments on the novels.

Wright, Andrew H. *Jane Austen's Novels: A Study in Structure*. New York: Oxford University Press, 1953. Individual chapters for the novels, with an emphasis on characters. A good summary of the criticism of Jane Austen and a very valuable annotated bibliography.

Articles: Collections

Heath, William, ed. *Discussions of Jane Austen*. Boston: D. C. Heath and Co., 1961. A collection of essays and reviews, including Jane Austen's correspondence with J. S. Clarke, Sir Walter Scott's review of *Emma*, and Charlotte Bronte's criticism.

Watt, Ian, ed. *Jane Austen: A Collection of Critical Essays*. Englewood Cliffs, N.J.: Prentice-Hall, Inc., 1963. Includes the valuable essays by Virginia Woolf, Reuben Brower, and D. W. Harding. The editor's preface is a valuable survey of Jane Austen's reputation and the various critical approaches to her works.

Individual Articles

Babb, Howard S. "Dialogue with Feeling: A Note on *Pride and Prejudice.*" *Kenyon Review.* xx (203-216). Emphasizes the emotional content which underlies the social dialogue.

Blueston, George. *Novels into Film.* Baltimore: the John Hopkins Press, 1957. An interesting chapter on *Pride and Prejudice,* showing the difficulties involved in translating the novel into a movie. A close analysis of the "Assembly Ball" sequence.

Bowen, Elizabeth. "Jane Austen." In *The English Novelists. A Survey of the Novel by Twenty Contemporary Novelists.* ed. Derek Verschoyle. New York: Harcourt, Brace and Co., 1936. An appreciative essay.

Branton, Clarence. "The Ordinations in Jane Austen's Novels." *Nineteenth-Century Fiction,* X (1955). 156-9. On the wrong date for Mr. Collins' ordination.

Brogan, Howard O. "Science and Narrative Structure in Austen, Hardy, and Woolf." *Nineteenth-Century Fiction,* XI (1957), 276-87. The cultural patterns in her novel reflect Newtonian science.

Brower, Reuben A. "The Controlling Hand: Jane Austen and *Pride and Prejudice.*" *Scrutiny,* XIII (1945), 99-111. The novelist is alert to the possibilities of meaning in any act, yet can make precise statements of character. Excellent analysis of Darcy's character.

Burchell, Samuel. "Jane Austen: Theme of Isolation." *Nineteenth-Century Fiction,* X (1955), 146-50. Essential theme of her novels is the loneliness of men and women. Darcy and Elizabeth cross the chasm which exists between people.

Daiches, David. "Jane Austen, Karl Marx, and the Aristocratic Dance." *American Scholar,* XVII (1948), 289-96. She sees the ruthless economic realities underlying the "graceful social dance," and was thus a Marxist before Marx.

Drew, Philip. "A Significant Incident in *Pride and Prejudice*." *Nineteenth-Century Fiction*, XIII (1959), 356-8. The reader's estimate of the hero is governed by the heroine's reaction to him.

Elsbree, Langdon. "Jane Austen and the Dance of Fidelity and Complaisance." *Nineteenth-Century Fiction*, XV (1960). 113-136. The movement of the novel as compared to a dance movement.

Fox, Robert C. "Elizabeth Bennet: Prejudice or Vanity?" *Nineteenth-Century Fiction*, XVII (1962), 185-7 Fundamental difference between Elizabeth and Darcy is between pride and vanity.

Forster, E. M. *Abinger Harvest*. New York: Meridian Books, 1955. Three brief reviews and essays by a confirmed "Jane Austenite."

Greene, D. J. "Jane Austen and the Peerage." *PMLA*, LXVIII (1953), 1017-31. On actual families behind the sub-royalty in her novels; says that the underlying theme of the novels is the rise of the middle class.

Halliday, E. M. "Narrative Perspective in *Pride and Prejudice*." *Nineteenth-Century Fiction*, XV (1960), 65-71. On the gradual predominance of Elizabeth as point of view in the novel. Excellent.

Leavis, Q. D. "A Critical Theory of Jane Austen's Writings, II," *Scrutiny*, X (1942), 272-294. Argues that *Pride and Prejudice* was written out of an earlier immature novel.

Marcus, Mordecai. "A Major Thematic Pattern in *Pride and Prejudice*." *Nineteenth-Century Fiction*, XVI (1961), 274-9. The pattern is the conflict between society and the individual, and the need to reconcile them for happiness.

Maugham, Somerset. *"Pride and Prejudice." Atlantic Monthly,*

CLXXXI, (May, 1948), 99-104. An appreciation of the novel.

Muir, Edwin. "Jane Austen and the Sense of Evil." *New York Times Book Review,* August 28, 1949. p. 1. Jane Austen as primarily a critic of conduct.

O'Connor, Frank. *Mirror in the Roadway.* New York: Alfred A. Knopf, 1956. An essay on Jane Austen, praising *Pride and Prejudice* as "impeccable" in its handling of the theme of imagination versus the judgment.

Parks, Edd. "A Human Failing in *Pride and Prejudice.*" *Nineteenth-Century Fiction,* X (1955), 237-40. On the money settlement to be arranged.

. . . . "Exegesis in Jane Austen's Novels." *South Atlantic Quarterly,* LI (1952), 103-119. Elizabeth provides the unity for the novel, helping to shape the reader's reactions.

. . . . "Jane Austen's Lure of the Next Chapter." *Nineteenth-Century Fiction,* VII (1952), 56-60. Each chapter is rounded but provides a corridor into the next chapter by leaving a problem to be solved.

Rathburn, Robert C. and Steinmann, Martin Jr. *From Jane Austen to Joseph Conrad.* Minneapolis: U. of Minnesota Press, 1958. Good introductory essay on her predecessors.

Schorer, Mark. "Pride Unprejudiced." *Kenyon Review,* XVIII (1956), 72-91. An interesting article on the discrepancy between aristrocratic assumptions of social place and bourgeois desire for social position in the novel.

Van Ghent, Dorothy. "Pride and Prejudice," in *The English Novel: Form and Function.* New York: Holt, Rinehart and Winston, 1953. Very good on the plot and language of the novel.

GLOSSARY OF LITERARY TERMS

Frequently Used in the Discussion of Jane Austen's Novels

Ambiguity—A quality in the style, or in the dramatic or fictional situation, which results in the reader's uncertainty as to its true meaning or significance. In passages of dialogue, for example, what one character actually means may be obscure due to the way in which he says something. A certain density and richness of meaning appears in Jane Austen's novels due to her ability to create ambiguity of dialogue and situation. The reader is called upon to interpret and weigh several possible meanings.

Apprenticeship novel—A special kind of novel which deals with the growth and maturing of the hero through a series of enlightening episodes. *Pride and Prejudice* has some elements of the "apprenticeship novel."

Archetype—A critical term referring to some large pattern into which a situation, a scene, or a character falls. Specific works of literature are said to please us primarily because they are examples of ageless "archetypes" which appeal to our unconscious selves. *Pride and Prejudice*, for example, is illustrative of the Cinderella archetype.

Architectonics—A term used in the discussion of the architecture or structure of any work of art. Jane Austen is said to be particularly careful about "constructing" or "structuring" her novels; that is, each element in her novel is carefully related to all other elements and takes its shape and emphasis from the needs of the whole work.

Attic—Referring to Attica, the province in Greece where Athens was located. Hence, any work of art is said to be "Attic" if, like a Jane Austen novel, it has the qualities of Athenian art, namely simplicity, clarity, calm, directness, order.

Augustan—Referring to the age of **Augustus**, the first Roman

Emperor, whose reign was noted for its intense literary and artistic activity. By extension, the term is applied to any such period of cultural ferment, most notably the England of the early and middle 18th century. During this time England was graced with the writing of Pope, Swift, Addison, Steele, Johnson, Gay, Fielding, Richardson and many others. Jane Austen is sometimes called "Augustan" because she equals the high standards of these predecessors and reflects many of their values.

Autobiographical fiction—Fiction which is largely dependent on autobiographical materials. It is still a matter of dispute whether Jane Austen's novels are largely based on autobiographical materials.

Bluestocking—A woman of any intellectual or literary pretension. Originally, the term was used in the late 18th century for a woman who attended congenial conversations or discussions of literary matters. Jane Austen is sometimes—wrongly—included in the group of "bluestockings" at this time.

Bon mot—Literally, a "good word"; that is, a clever saying. Jane Austen's dialogue is replete with "bons mots."

Characterization—The creation of credible human beings in fiction or drama. Fictional characters may be classified, first of all, as either "static" or "dynamic." Static characters are fictional characters who do not change in the course of the novel; dynamic characters do change (Elizabeth is a good example). Fictional characters may also be divided into "rounds" and "flats"; round characters are complex (such as Darcy or Elizabeth) while flat characters are simple, one-dimensional (such as Lydia or Lady Catherine). Jane Austen is a master of characterization.

Classic, classical—Adjectives used to indicate certain qualities in a work of art. A work is said to be "classical" if it has such qualities as balance, objectivity, clarity, directness, and order. Jane Austen's novels are often said to be "classical."

Comedy—A usually light light form of literature which attempts to provoke smiles and laughter and usually ends happily. It often has as its subject matter the eccentricities of special types of people (e.g. Collins as a typical incompetent parson) or certain aspects of society (e.g. Lady Catherine de Bourgh as a spokesman for the values of society).

Comedy of manners—Commedy which is mainly concerned with the foibles and ideas of high society. Frequently the plot deals with the troubles of young lovers, both of whom are witty and gifted in dialogue. The comedy of manners clearly has some influence on Jane Austen's novels.

Confidant, confidante—The close friends of hero and heroine, in whom they confide. Charlotte is Elizabeth's confidante; Bingley is probably Darcy's confidant.

Convention—A familiar artistic device or pattern which an artist uses and shapes in his own way. Jane Austen uses numerous conventions in her novel but inspires them with a new life. For example, the elopement is a familiar convention in the 18th century novel; Jane Austen uses it in the story of Lydia and Wickham. The figure of the tyrannical dowager appears again and again in literature; Jane Austen uses the convention in the figure of Lady Catherine.

Detachment.—An artist is said to be "detached" or illustrate the quality of "detachment" when he does not reveal his personality in the work of art, either by giving his own opinions directly or permitting his own emotions to show. Detachment is one feature of "classical" art, such as Jane Austen's novels.

Dialogue—The reproduction of conversation in drama or in fiction. Dialogue may be of little value in some novels (such as in Richardson or Faulkner) or of great importance in other novels (such as those by Jane Austen or Hemingway).

Diction—The kind of words used by a speaker or a writer. Diction in Jane Austen's novels is very important because the kind of words used by any character is an indicator of character (See Collins' letter in I, 13).

Didacticism—"Preachiness" in a work of literature. Literature written primarily to preach or inculcate a moral lesson is said to be "didactic." Since every piece of literature has some intellectual or moral content, arguments may arise as to whether a particular work of art (such as a novel by Jane Austen) is primarily didactic.

Dramatic irony—What a character says may be seen in one way by himself and in another way by the reader, because the reader has more information (and is less directly involved in the fictional events) than the character. This creates "dramatic irony." In Chapter 43, for example, when Mrs. Reynolds says that she does not know when her master, Mr. Darcy, will marry, since "I do not know who is good enough for him," her speech is innocent enough for her (she is innocently praising him); for Elizabeth, who dislikes Darcy, the speech carries certain overtones which the attentive reader cannot miss.

Epistolary novel—A novel written entirely by means of epistles—letters—among the main characters. The epistolary novel was extremely popular in the late 18th century, and shows its influence in *Pride and Prejudice* in the number of letters used there.

Form—The structure, shape, or organization of any work of art. Some works of art (especially novels) seem to be formless, being propelled mainly by the force of the novelist's personality. Other novels, such as those by Jane Austen, seem to be more organized, have more balance, proportion, or shape.

High Comedy—Comedy of a serious nature, based more on words, dialogue, ideas and intellectual content, rather than on physical comedy such as may be found in farce and low comedy.

Irony—A type of writing or speaking where what is meant is the opposite of what is said. Jane Austen's novels are shot through with irony of all kinds (See the discussion of the famous first sentence of the novel, I, i). Other kinds of irony which may be used are dramatic irony, irony of situation. Jane Austen is widely praised for her ironic view of life.

Minor plot (also subplot)—A plot of secondary interest in a drama or novel. This does not mean that the minor plot is irrelevant; in fact, the minor plot, in a well-ordered piece of literature, should contribute to the main theme and the total effect of the work. For example, the love-marriage theme of the Darcy-Elizabeth plot is supported by the minor plots of Jane and Bingley, Lydia and Wickham, Charlotte, and Collins.

Moral sense—The quality in a work of art which indicates the degree of the artist's interest in morality. Whereas some authors may interest themselves in politics, sociology, religion, or metaphysics, others, such as Jane Austen, seem largely concerned with the problem of right conduct in society, and the differences between right and wrong in certain situations (e.g. Lydia's elopement). Jane Austen is said to have a strong "moral sense."

Motif—A simple element which serves as a foundation for the themes and subject matter of a work of art. Marriage is the main motif of *Pride and Prejudice*, and it is presented in a number of ways.

Neoclassicism—Literally, "new classicism." The culture of the 17th and 18th centuries attempted to base itself on the values (real or imagined) of the classical cultures of Greece and Rome. The works of art were "neoclassical" to the extent that they succeeded in emulating the ideals of the "classic" or "classical."

Norms—Standards or models of right conduct or taste. Jane Austen is interested in the norms established by reasonable people, and satirizes anyone who deviates from those norms.

Novel of manners—A novel which is largely concerned with portraying the customs, standards, and conventions of a particular society at a particular time and place. Jane Austen is often considered to be one of the novelists of manners in English literature.

Novel of character—A novel concerned mainly with character, rather than with plot, or plot incident. There are relatively few major incidents in *Pride and Prejudice;* most of the novel is concerned with the development of the major characters.

Objectivity—The quality of disinterestedness in a novelist. A novelist is said to be objective if he keeps his personal attitudes, sentiments, and emotions out of the work. If he is like Jane Austen, he will allow the main characters to act for themselves, reveal themselves, without appearing to manipulate them.

Plot device—A situation or conventional plot incident which has been used by many writers, e.g. the elopement device was commonplace in the 18th century novel and drama.

Rake—A wastrel, or immoral young man. A familiar figure in 17th and 18th century plays and novels (e.g. Lovelace in *Clarissa*). He is frequently used in the plot as someone who is "reformed" by the goodness, good sense, and purity of the heroine. Darcy has some elements of the traditional "rake" figure.

Recognition—A "recognition" plot is one in which the main event, or scene, involves the recognition by the major character of some fact which he has not known before (The plot of Sophocles' *Oedipus* is the classic example). Elizabeth's "recognition" of Darcy's true character, after reading his letter, makes *Pride and Prejudice* a novel of recognition.

Repartee—Clever and witty response or retort in dialogue; witty conversation. Some of the dialogue between Elizabeth and Darcy is a good example of repartee.

Restraint.—A work of art is said to display "restraint" when it remains calm, deliberate, well-organized, rather than emotional or personally effusive.

Satire—A mode of literature which uses humor or comedy to criticize humanity at large, or society specifically, for the purposes of effecting some change. Satire may be harsh (as in Jonathan Swift's writings) or gentle (as in Jane Austen's novels). In any case, it is pragmatic, realistic, affirmative.

Self-effacing author—An author who erases his own personality, preventing its entrance into the novel, permitting the reader to draw his own conclusions about the dramatic scene (see *Detachment, Objectivity*).

Sensibility—Emotionalism in matters of taste and conduct. In the 18th century, there was a tendency to assert that man's feelings were proper guides in aesthetics, morality, and religion. "Sensibility" was thus an important part of the growing "romantic movement." Jane Austen was one of those who opposed the newer ways of thinking, preferring rather the dictates of Reason and calm deliberation.

Stock character—A conventional character type which reappears in many works of art. The bumbling parson, the man-hungry young girl, the silly mother, the preposterous dowager are all stock characters which Jane Austen uses for her own purposes.

Stock situation—A conventional situation found in many works of art. In *Pride and Prejudice,* poor girl—meets—rich boy is a stock situation, but of course transmuted into something fresh and meaningful.

Style—The arrangement of words into sentences and larger patterns so as to express the personality of the speaker or writer. Jane Austen is everywhere concerned with style in the writing or speaking of her characters. A large part of her characterization is achieved through a careful treatment of their styles. The reader in turn must be sensitive to matters of style in reading a novel of Jane Austen; in *Pride and Prejudice* style is effectively used to characterize all the characters, notably Lydia, Mrs. Bennet, Lady Catherine, Collins.

Tradition—The body of conventional materials which an author inherits from his predecessors, including the stock characters, situations, motifs, themes, and aesthetic values. An important question for any critic or serious student is to what extent does Jane Austen participate in the tradition of the 18th century novel.

Understatement—A kind of irony in which what is said does not really suggest the importance of the subject. Numerous examples appear in the ironic writing of Jane Austen. For example, in Chapter 41 Elizabeth tells Wickham that she has seen Darcy at Pemberley and "he is very much what he ever was." Wickham is disturbed by the real meaning of what she has said, and eventually leaves unsatisfied.